ASPECTS OF BIOGRAPHY

ASPECTS OF BIOGRAPHY

BY

ANDRÉ MAUROIS

Translated from the French
by
S. C. ROBERTS

CAMBRIDGE
AT THE UNIVERSITY PRESS
1929

To

SIR J. J. THOMSON, O.M.

Master of Trinity College

Cambridge

CAMBRIDGE
UNIVERSITY PRESS

University Printing House, Cambridge CB2 8BS, United Kingdom

Cambridge University Press is part of the University of Cambridge.

It furthers the University's mission by disseminating knowledge in the pursuit of education, learning and research at the highest international levels of excellence.

www.cambridge.org
Information on this title: www.cambridge.org/9781107437586

First published 1929
First paperback edition 2014

A catalogue record for this publication is available from the British Library

ISBN 978-1-107-43758-6 Paperback

CONTENTS

PREFACE

THIS book is based on six lectures given at Trinity College, Cambridge, in May 1928, on the Clark foundation. Mr E. M. Forster, who had given the lectures in the preceding year, had taken as his subject "Aspects of the Novel." Accordingly, I chose a complementary subject and, following his example, made no attempt to trace the history of a literary form.

The reader who wants such a history may find it either in Professor Waldo H. Dunn's *English Biography*, or in Mr Harold Nicolson's *Development of English Biography*, or, in a very brief but excellent form, in *From Plutarch to Strachey*, by Professor Cross, of Yale.

Perhaps I ought to explain why lectures delivered in English now appear in the form of a translation. When I found that the notes I had used at Trinity needed to be entirely re-cast for publication in book form, I chose to make the revision in French and Mr Roberts has been good enough to translate this revised version into English.

A. M.

February 1929.

CHAPTER ONE

MODERN BIOGRAPHY

Chapter I

MODERN BIOGRAPHY

STANDING in my place last year, Mr E. M. Forster began his lectures by invoking the memory of Clark: first with a prayer that he might dispense his integrity and sound learning to the assembled company; secondly with a petition that he would accord to the speaker a certain measure of inattention: "For," he said, "I am not keeping quite strictly to the terms laid down—'Period or periods of English Literature.' This condition, though it sounds liberal and is liberal enough in spirit, happens verbally not quite to suit our subject."

For my own part, I should like to begin by invoking Mr Forster and by thanking him for having thus shown me the way and set me the example of indiscipline. Had it not been for him, I should have tried to give you a scholarly, chronological account of the history of biography in England. I should have told you that about 690 Adamnan, the Irish saint and historian, wrote *The Life of Saint Columba*, a highly-praised work which has been described as the most exhaustive piece of biographical writing to be found in European literature not only of that early period but of the whole of the Middle Ages. I should then have passed to *The Life of Alfred the Great*, written by Asser, who, so far as I can gather from his commentators, is willing to talk of anything but his hero, thereby establishing himself as ancestor and precursor of most modern biographers. I should have given a disquisition on Walton and on Johnson. Then I should have come to Boswell and should have told you that he was the creator of modern biography—that would have been a mistake, but a mistake transformed into a truism by its antiquity. I should have composed an extravagant eulogy of Boswell, of his acute understanding and his delicate psychology. I should have twitted those who have taken him for a fool and I should have quoted the remark: "A wiser man than Macaulay, James Boswell." Or perhaps I should, on the contrary, have denied talent to Boswell and have tried to prove that what we have taken for genius is nothing but a prodigious *naïveté* which flatters our conceit by its simplicity. In a discourse on Victorian biography I should have delivered a panegyric of Moore and Lockhart; I should have spoken of Trevelyan's *Macaulay*, of Forster's *Dickens*, of Lewes' *Goethe*; in passing, I should have rehabilitated

Froude; a final lecture on Mr Strachey, Mr Nicolson and their imitators would have rounded off a bird's-eye view of English biography. I should have taught you nothing, for you know more of these subjects than I; but perhaps I should have won for myself that peace of mind which comes to a man who has obeyed the rules.

Yes, I should have prepared these lectures with all the ease of commonplace if I had not read *Aspects of the Novel*. But having read Mr Forster and, in particular, his fine comparison between true scholarship, which is and always has been the pride of this university, and that pseudo-scholarship which is but a foolish travesty of it, I said to myself that since circumstances had not made me a professional scholar, I must beware of the absurdity of playing the pseudo-scholar. Even so, in January last I almost let myself be tempted. "Yes," I thought, "the whole of Cambridge knows all this, but perhaps I could put fresh life into a well-worn subject by giving it a new form"; and, for want of another means of handling the subject, I was ready to give myself up, like a tired and clumsy swimmer, to the chronological current when towards the end of the month I was saved by Mr Harold Nicolson. Mr Nicolson, himself a real scholar, published this year a small book to which he gave the title *The Development of English Biography*. In this book he had done exactly what I was contemplating myself; and he had done it to such perfection that there was not a word left for me to say. So this time I was forced, willy-nilly, to abandon the easy high-road, to give up the lives of St Columba and of Alfred the Great and to find some other means of presenting the subject of biography to you.

Furthermore, what interests you and me is not a recitation of all the works which, "depuis deux mille ans qu'il y a des Anglais et qui écrivent," have been devoted to the records of human lives; for the problem is not merely a historical one. Looked at all round, it is an ethical problem and an aesthetic problem.

Is there such a thing as modern biography? Is there a literary form different from that of the traditional biography? Are its methods legitimate or ought they to be abandoned? Ought biography to be an art or a science? Can it, like the novel, be a means of expression, a means of escape for the author as well as for the reader? Such are some of the questions which we shall be able to examine together; and that we may be loyal to the spirit of this foundation, our examples will be taken from English literature.

First of all, is there a type of biography which we may call 'modern,' having certain specific and permanent characteristics which differentiate it from the biographies of an earlier age? On this question English literary opinion is at present somewhat divided. The word 'modern' is a source of irritation to a large number of worthy and intelligent English people. Literary movements, like political movements, are oscillatory. After a strong reaction against Victorianism, the pendulum has, very naturally, swung back.

In 1918 Mr Lytton Strachey could write:

> The art of biography seems to have fallen on evil times in England.... Those two fat volumes, with which it is our custom to commemorate the dead—who does not know them, with their ill-digested masses of material, their slipshod style, their tone of tedious panegyric, their lamentable lack of selection, of detachment, of design? They are as familiar as the *cortège* of the undertaker, and wear the same air of slow, funereal barbarism.

This verdict, moreover, was approved in England

by the majority of those who read it. Would it still be approved in 1928? I do not think so. Your most advanced critics now display a mischievous air of learning in praising the genius, the artless profusion of the great Victorian biographers. They are willing to maintain that, all things considered, their methods were the soundest.

This reaction has no doubt had its value. The Victorians had established certain conventions upon which a stable, and perhaps a happy, society had lived. Out of this very stability and happiness there sprang a doubt of the value of the conventions, and the whole of a later generation became used to regarding them as foolish, and rather ridiculous, survivals. In fact they were, like all human institutions, at once admirable and ridiculous. It was well for admiration to have its turn and then to be merged into humour.

But we may quite sincerely admire the qualities of one type of biography and at the same time admit the existence of another. Read a page of a Victorian biography and then read a page of Mr Strachey. You will see immediately that you have before you two very different types. A book by Trevelyan or by Lockhart, apart from being constructed as perfectly as it can be, is above all things a document; a book by Mr Strachey is above all things a work of art. Undoubtedly Mr Strachey is at the same time an exact historian; but he has the power of presenting his material in a perfect art-form, and it is this form which is for him the first essential.

What is true of the great writers of each of the two periods is true also of those lesser authors, who, in an attempt to exploit a literary success, imagined that they had only to employ the same methods in order to produce a masterpiece.

> "The manner of Macaulay," writes Mr Desmond MacCarthy, "was soon discredited by imitators who had no learning to support it; Mr Lytton Strachey, too, has not been blessed in his literary descendants, the majority of whom ape his methods without understanding his discretion. The form he made fashionable is one which requires the finest literary tact and minute research."

But, whether Victorian or modern, these imitators, while they display the common characteristic of being detestable writers, group themselves into very distinct classes. A bad Victorian biography is a formless mass of ill-digested matter; a bad modern biography is a book of spurious fame animated by a would-be ironic spirit which is merely cruel and shallow. Good or bad, there is such a thing as 'modern biography.'

We may ask when the old biography ceased to exist and modern biography came into being. Virginia Woolf and Harold Nicolson are almost in agreement about the date of the change. Harold Nicolson says 1907. Virginia Woolf feels herself in a position to state that in December 1910, or about that time, human nature suffered a change:

> I am not saying that one went out, as one might into a garden, and there saw that a rose had flowered, or that a hen had laid an egg. The change was not sudden and definite like that. But a change there was, nevertheless; and, since one must be arbitrary, let us date it about the year 1910. The first signs of it are recorded in the books of Samuel Butler, in *The Way of All Flesh* in particular; the plays of Bernard Shaw continue to record it. In life one can see the change, if I may use a homely illustration, in the character of one's cook. The Victorian cook lived like a Leviathan in the lower depths, formidable, silent, obscure, inscrutable; the Georgian cook is a creature of sunshine and fresh air....Do you ask for more solemn instances of the power of the human race to change?...All human relations have shifted—those between masters and servants,

husbands and wives, parents and children. And when human relations change there is at the same time a change in religion, conduct, politics, and literature. Let us agree to place one of these changes about the year 1910.

It is a passage at once alluring and provocative.

"Don't you see," a hundred Englishmen will reply, "that the very exactitude of this paradox proves its absurdity? No, human nature hasn't changed; it can't change. Human passions remain the same. The relations of master to servant, of parent to child undergo certain superficial and temporary modifications, but very soon deeper causes restore the right and proper relationships. The change is merely on the face of things and it is just because you magnify these slight variations on the surface and neglect the deep and abiding qualities that you produce fantastic novels and biographies which are cruel, unjust and sterile."

Personally, I have a great admiration for Virginia Woolf and I freely admit that her attitude in the passage which I have quoted is deliberately paradoxical. But paradox is not always in the wrong. Certainly, human nature changes but slowly; it is none the less true that in the history of the human race there have been certain rare periods in which vast revolutions have been effected in a very short time. One may give as an example the passing of the freedom of thought of the Greek philosophers into the theological thought of the Middle Ages; or again, in the time first of Bacon and then of Descartes, the passing of this theological thought into the first beginnings of formulated, scientific thought.

So it appears that in England, as elsewhere, the human race, about the beginning of the twentieth century, passed through one of these periods of intellectual revolution. What are the characteristics by which we shall recognise the period which was our own?

The first is the invasion of the sphere of psychology and ethics by the intellectual methods of the man of learning. There is no subject (excepting the Absolute, as Mallarmé would have said) on which a young man of 1910, much less a young man of 1928, would ask himself: "What am I obliged to believe?" Whatever the question, he is prepared to examine it himself in a courageous spirit and to accept the results of his investigation. He will not shrink from any of the intellectual consequences to which his researches may lead him. That this spirit of free enquiry which is characteristic of the young generation has a profound influence upon your novelists is obvious. Compare, for instance, the freedom of Mr Forster or of Mr Aldous Huxley or of the Sitwells with the deliberately-imposed moral restraint of Dickens or Thackeray. Nor has its effect been less upon history and upon that particular branch of history which is biography.

The modern biographer, if he is honest, will not allow himself to think: "Here is a great king, a great statesman, a great writer; round his name a legend has been built; it is on the legend, and on the legend alone, that I wish to dwell." No. He thinks rather: "Here is a man. I possess a certain number of documents, a certain amount of evidence about him. I am going to attempt to draw a true portrait. What will this portrait be? I have no idea. I don't want to know before I have actually drawn it. I am prepared to accept whatever a prolonged contemplation of my subject may reveal to me, and to correct it in proportion to such new facts as I discover." Think of Byron, for instance: compare Moore's portrait of him with that drawn by Mr Harold Nicolson in *The*

Last Journey; to every impartial observer it is evident that Mr Nicolson has a much greater regard for truth than Moore.

Our own age has formed for itself an exact conception of truth comparable with that conception of scientific truth which Professor Karl Pearson has expounded in his *Grammar of Science*. We will not let the biographer have his judgments dictated to him by preconceived ideas; we demand that the observation of facts, and nothing else, shall lead to the expression of general ideas, and that these general ideas shall afterwards be verified by fresh and independent research, conducted with care and without passion. We want all the documents to be used if they throw light upon a new aspect of the subject; neither fear, nor admiration, nor hostility must lead the biographer to neglect or to pass over a single one of them in silence.

I am well aware that even scholars are not always free from violent affections. One sees them in love with a system because they have invented it; one recalls the tragic history of the physicist who devoted himself for ten years to the observation of rays which did not exist. The historian cannot always preserve the spirit of free enquiry and the biographer still less; he is human; his heroes may inspire him with a love, or a hatred, which will sometimes warp his judgment. Sometimes he may be fired by religious, sometimes by ethical passion. It would be absurd to imagine the modern biographer as a completely impartial being. But I think we may say that it is more rarely now than formerly that we see him undertake the task in the interests of a family or of friends.

"The Victorian biographer," says Virginia Woolf, "was dominated by the idea of goodness. Noble, upright, chaste, severe; it is thus that the Victorian worthies are presented to us. The figure is almost always above life-size in top-hat and frock-coat, and the manner of presentation becomes increasingly clumsy and laborious."

Custom and the family combined to insist upon this conventional treatment:

"In America in the nineteenth century," says William Roscoe Thayer, "when any distinguished citizen, lawyer, judge, merchant or writer died, it was taken for granted that his clergyman, if he had one, would write his life, unless his wife, sister, or cousin was preferred."

Prudent men chose their biographers before they

died, just as they appointed their executors. Sometimes these choices were regrettable. Carlyle, for instance, found in Froude an intimate and dangerous enemy. The Prince Consort and Cardinal Manning were made ridiculous by two exceedingly well-meaning biographers. Other choices were happier: that of Monypenny and Buckle, for instance, by Lord Beaconsfield's heirs; that of Mr Charles Whibley by the family of Lord John Manners.

But, in the old Victorian biographies, the quality most appreciated by the families of the heroes was the respect of propriety. The man's private life, his daily occupations, his follies, his faults were to be passed over in silence. If his life had been notoriously scandalous, only vague allusions were to be made[1].

"What business," says Tennyson, "has the public to know about Byron's wildnesses? He has given them fine work and they ought to be satisfied."

The author saw a mass of instructions placed at his disposal: letters, account-books, private diaries. Such generosity bound him to a strict rule of loyalty. He was charged to prove himself discreet and laudatory. If there was a widow, she kept a careful watch both upon the portrait of her husband and upon the

[1] C. Trueblood.

attitude which she wished to see herself assume before the eyes of posterity. The results are only too familiar: "books so well stuffed with virtues," as someone said, "that I began to doubt the very existence of virtue."

Suddenly, into the peaceful aisles where these heavily-draped monuments were accumulating, Mr Strachey introduced first *Eminent Victorians* and then *Queen Victoria*. Side by side with the stone statues of the nineteenth century stood these exquisitely ironical terra-cottas—astonishing, charming. Everything about them was different from the traditional type. The Victorian biographers had recorded the lives of heroes whom they unreservedly admired; they had chosen them on account of this very admiration. Mr Strachey seemed almost to have chosen his because he did not unreservedly admire them.

"A point of view," he writes in a recent article, "by no means implies sympathy. One might almost say that this choice implies the reverse. At any rate it is curious to observe how many instances there are of great historians who were at daggers drawn with their subject."

And he shows that Gibbon, one of the most highly

civilised people who ever lived, chose a barbarous period for his history, and that Michelet, a republican and a romantic, never showed himself a finer historian than in dealing with the period of Louis XIV. It is a remark which applies marvellously well to Mr Strachey himself. He has chosen the Victorian era because temperamentally he is in strong reaction against Victorianism. He is no longer the sculptor of funerary monuments, he is the perfect painter of posthumous portraits, with just a touch—a very light touch—of caricature.

There is nothing ponderous about Mr Strachey's method. He does not criticise, he does not judge—he exposes. His procedure is that of the great humorists. The author never appears himself. He walks behind the queen, behind Cardinal Manning, behind General Gordon; with faithful exactitude he reproduces their gestures and their tricks of speech and so obtains excellent comic effects.

His imitation of the queen's mannerisms, of her underlining all the words of a phrase, of her writing "Lord M—" instead of "Lord Melbourne," "Dear Albert" instead of "Prince Albert"—all these little details produce a very natural and human picture. Even the quotation of an official document sometimes gives rather a cruelly humorous effect. For instance, when he comes to the building of the Albert Memorial, Mr Strachey does not tell us that it is an ugly monument: he simply describes it as it is, using the architect's own words.

Such a method, when used by Mr Strachey, Mr Nicolson and some others, produces fine work since the writers are too good artists not to realise the importance of an artistic change being effected with scrupulous delicacy. But if, on the other hand, it is applied by writers lacking in human sympathy and in psychological perception, its effects are simply those of rather low comedy. Some of Mr Strachey's disciples who do not share his profound knowledge of men and things have quite frankly used his recipes. Instead of choosing as the heroes of their biographies "great men, so that we might imitate their virtues, they have been content with contemptible men, so that we might laugh at their follies." Some of these books make one regret the old *Life and Letters* in two volumes which, after all, was a very useful piece of research, and sometimes the reader is very naturally wearied by "that insolent manner of pulling dead lions by the beard."

Even when controlled by artistic feeling, by

moderation and by good taste, the modern biographer's attitude has often been condemned, and condemned by people of intelligence. Critics and professional historians have said: "Perhaps the traditional figures which have been drawn for us—the Wellington of English, the Washington of American legend—were not true figures. That may well be, but what does it matter to us? It is not good to tell the whole truth. Very often we know some cruel story about a living friend which we are very careful not to repeat. Why should we show less loyalty towards our dead friends and towards great men? Of course they were not perfect; of course there was a legendary element in the superfine portrait that had been painted of them. But was not this legend a source of inspiration? It served as an example to men and raised them above their own level.

Moreover, was the portrait really so false? A man's deeds are often greater than the man himself. No one is a great man to his valet. That does not prove that there are no great men; it proves that there are very few great valets.

It is quite possible to discover and to record defamatory anecdotes about a writer of genius or a statesman, but is he, when thus revealed, more truly an ordinary man than the hero whom a whole people has seen in him? Perhaps the hero was nothing but a mask, but cannot the mask become the real personality? It was Mr Max Beerbohm who, in *The Happy Hypocrite*, told the story of the *roué* who, to seduce a young girl, put on the mask of an innocent young man; in the end his face became like the mask. 'Plutarch lied,' wrote a brilliant French pamphleteer after the war. Perhaps it is true, but is it not a good thing that Plutarch lied so well?"

For a reply to this question of loyalty towards one's hero, one may quote Doctor Johnson: "The value of every story," he said, "depends on its being true. A story is a picture either of an individual, or of human nature in general: if it be false, it is a picture of nothing." Of course there may be cases in which it is painful to tell the truth, whether out of respect towards a dead friend or because it would offend a wife or children still living. In such a case the solution is simple. The life must not be written. If it is written, it must be truly written.

Mr Strachey would have little difficulty in defending himself on the score of the value of legend in the formation of the reader's character. Certainly, it is a wholly admirable thing to put lofty examples before men, and especially before young men, but they will not strive to imitate them unless these models are true to life. The biography of standardised panegyric had no educative value, because no one any longer believed in it. A generation trained to respect scientific truth demanded sincerity in a biographer before it would give itself up to enthusiasm. Moreover, the greatness of a character comes home the more closely in proportion as we feel the character to be human and akin to our own. If someone who shares our own weaknesses has, by an effort of his own will, attained to glory or to sainthood, we feel ourselves encouraged and perhaps improved. But who would wish to imitate the attitudes of a statue carved in stone?

Besides, it would be untrue to say that a method such as Mr Strachey's takes away all greatness from his heroes.

The General Gordon whom he has drawn for us, and even his Prince Albert, are figures with a certain nobility and win our sympathy. As for Queen Victoria, Mr Strachey may perhaps have begun his book with ironical intentions, but he finished it with a portrait full of dignity and simple poetry. It was one of you who told me the other day that the most remarkable phenomenon of modern biography was the conquest of Mr Strachey by Queen Victoria. Mr Strachey has demonstrated not that the hero is an ordinary man, but that an ordinary man or woman can become a hero or a heroine. This seems to me to be a healthy enough notion for the reader. If I were one of Strachey's heroes, it would please me better to be loved for what I truly was, good and bad mixed together, than for a soul more beautiful than mine could ever have been.

Walt Whitman has said some good things on this subject:

Now, there's Abraham Lincoln: people get to know his traits, his habits of life, some of his characteristics set off in the most positive relief; soon all sorts of stories are fathered on him—some of them true, some of them apocryphal—volumes of stories (stories decent and indecent); legitimate stories, illegitimate; and so Lincoln comes to us more or less falsified. Yet I know that the hero is after all greater than any idealisation. Undoubtedly—just as the man is greater than his portrait—the landscape than the picture of it—the fact, than anything we can know about the fact.... I often reflect, how very different every fellow must have been from the fellow we come upon in the myths—with the surroundings, the incidents, the push and pull of the concrete moment, all left out as wrongly set forth. It is hard to extract a man's real self—any man—from such a chaotic man—from such historic débris.

And the man who was to Whitman what Boswell was to Johnson—Traubel—has noted this:

Whitman said to me to-night again as he has before: "Some day you will be writing about me: be sure to write about me honest: whatever you do, do not prettify me: include all the hells and damns." Adding: "I have hated so much of the biography in literature because it is so untrue: look at our national figures how they are spoilt by liars, by the people who think they can improve on God Almighty's work—who put on an extra touch here, there, here again, there again, until the real man is no longer recognisable."

Whitman is right: the biographer who imagines that he can improve upon nature by modifying the element of the ridiculous in great men, by omitting a love-letter written in a moment of weakness, by denying a change of front or of doctrine, such a biographer mutilates, distorts and, in the last analysis, belittles his hero. There is only one more dangerous kind of biographer, the kind that suppresses or diminishes the elements of greatness and of moral beauty in his subject.

We have tried to define the first characteristic of modern biography: "the courageous search for truth." But a taste for truth would be an inadequate formula for the characterisation either of modern biography or of our own age; for this is not the first time that a sceptical humanity has refused to accept a distortion of truth. It was the same in the time of the Greeks and again at the time of the Renaissance; yet the form of biography which interests us was not produced in those periods. The characters of Plutarch and of Vasari, the great biographer of the Renaissance painters, are never complete men, true men. Why?

It would seem that the writers of our own day possess in a greater degree than their predecessors a sense of the complexity and mobility of human beings and in a lesser degree a sense of their unity.

Such an attitude can be explained, on the one hand, by the revival of the old philosophies of mobility by Bergson and his school; on the other hand by the progress of modern physics and biology which behind the comparatively simple constructions of an earlier age—when the atom and the cell seemed to be indivisible units making up the whole body—have discovered new universes, infinitely small, but as complex as those in which they are themselves contained.

The psychologist has in this matter followed the lead of the physicist. Formerly it was believed that in the human spirit there had also been discovered indivisible atoms. Characters and passions had been defined; one man was good, another was wicked; Dickens was a domestic man, Byron was a Don Juan.

Behind these simply-constructed characters the modern historian seeks for the tissue, almost invisible but still there, which holds them together. As soon as he looks into it more deeply he finds a mysterious life often ignored even by the man who has been the subject of it.

No doubt the Freudian system has been pressed too far and perhaps too much emphasis has been placed upon the Unconscious—a badly defined term in any event—in the explanation of character, and that at the expense of human will and freedom. But we have realised that a human being or a human event is a more complex amalgam than was ever believed before.

In the same way that, in order to explain observed phenomena in physics, we must visualise the atoms as systems of electrons, revolving round a central nucleus, so to understand an individual character we must realise that it is made up of diverse personalities which are sometimes massed together and sometimes follow each other within it. There is not only the real self—in itself very difficult to define—with which we think we come face to face when we honestly examine ourselves; there is also what a moment ago we called the mask. In Disraeli, for instance, the mask was the completely-detached cynic; the real man was shy. There is the personality that others see, varying according to the spectator, since we show to each one of our friends a fresh facet of our character. The Byron described by Shelley was not the Byron described by Trelawny or Lady Blessington or Claire Clairmont—though no one of them was lacking in sincerity. "Do I contradict myself?" says Walt Whitman again. "Very well, I contradict myself, I contain multitudes."

The modern man believes that it is impossible to understand anything of the psychology of a human being without examining its different facets and without going into infinitely small detail. In the French novel Proust has given us this analysis of detail and I suspect that he has exerted a wide influence on your own novelists.

In history we all admit that events which had previously been explained as due to a simple cause or to some great character are in fact the sum of a thousand tiny actions and expressions of will. Consider, for instance, how many theories on the subject of the American Revolution and the War of Independence have been completely changed in recent years. In biography we recognise that a man is not a solid mass of virtues or of vices, that we are not concerned with passing a moral judgment upon him and further, that he does not remain the same man from early manhood to old age. In Proust, Saint-Loup is at first a fine character; in the end he becomes something very much like his monstrous uncle, M. de Charlus; in the same way it is possible that Disraeli, after beginning life with serious defects of character, may have completed it in a serenity which lacks neither greatness nor beauty.

It would hardly be true to say that it has been realised in every age that man is a complex being. Certainly a Montaigne in France and a Shakespeare in England knew as well as Proust the complexity of human nature; but after them two influences came into play: on the one side the Reformation, with its theory of predestination, discouraged the possibilities of change in human personality; on the other, the classical psychologists of the seventeenth century in France, by their creation of abstract characters, necessarily conceived of them as simpler. Compare, for instance, the complexity, the delicate shades, of a character such as that of Hamlet, with the relatively simple characters of Corneille. Mr Nicolson has very justly noted this destructive influence of the French moralists of the seventeenth century and, in general, of the 'character' method on biography:

> The popularity of the Theophrastian character sketch gave method and unity to psychological investigation. But its influence was in other ways harmful; it led biographers to fix upon a certain quality or type, and subsequently so to adjust the details as to fix them into the thesis or frame selected. This deductive method, which is opposed to the inductive realism of our natural genius, can be recognised in many of the historical portraits of the period, and it is this which prevents Walton's *Lives* from attaining to the perfection of pure biography.

The influence of this classical psychology which,

for ethical reasons, was obliged to admit that man does not change, was maintained throughout the eighteenth, and even through the greater part of the nineteenth century. The romantic Byronian surrenders himself to the tragic element in his character; he goes further and believes that no other character presents the same tragic unity. A personality such as Byron's seems astonishing to us because he is so little conscious of the true cause of his passions. There is no self-analysis; he makes no attempt, as Meredith does, to change his character; he accepts it and makes the mistake of regarding it as homogeneous. It is not until much later that the idea begins to emerge again, with the great Russian writers and in particular with Dostoievsky, of a multiplicity of vital energy at the heart of a single soul. Next comes the analysis of Proust which reduces the whole idea of personality to dust. At the end of this analysis there is apparently nothing left by which to recognise a man save his name, his body, his clothes and a few external mannerisms. Below these the development of personality is going on—that is, a succession of states and feelings, grouped together but not united, and giving man the appearance of resembling those colonies of marine animals which live at the bottom of the sea. He is a colony of feelings, a coral-reef of diverse personalities.

Is such a picture of humanity a fair one? No picture of humanity is fair. What is true of man, as of all natural phenomena, is that he is subject to certain rhythms. Sometimes he is more especially conscious of his complexity; sometimes, on the other hand, he realises that he has no social value unless he can impress a unity upon himself, even though it be an artificial one. At this particular moment of his history it is the feeling of complexity which is dominant, and we may record as the second modern characteristic, the insistence on the complexity of personality[1].

There remains a third. The modern man does not look in a biography for exactly what the seventeenth-century man was seeking. The man of classical training, hedged about by a stricter system of religious and ethical teaching and deriving a more solid support from it, sought above all in the books which

[1] On the whole of this subject see Ramón Fernandez, *Messages* (N.R.F.) and *Introduction à l'étude de la personnalité* (Au Sans Pareil).

he read for a confirmation of this attitude. Hence his taste for moral treatises, for meditations, for biographies in the manner of Plutarch. The modern man is more restless. Troubled by his instincts, deprived in many instances of the firm faith which might help him to resist them, worried by his analytical habits of mind, he longs, in the course of his reading of fiction or of history, to find brothers who share his troubles. He longs to believe that others have known the struggles which he endures, the long and painful meditations in which he himself has indulged. So he is grateful to those more human biographies for showing him that even the hero is a divided being. Plato conceived of the human soul as perpetually drawn by two horses, one white and the other black, one dragging him up towards the highest, the other dragging him down to the lowest in his nature. For several centuries humanity was forced to forget the existence of the black charger. Perhaps our own age denies the existence of the white horse a little too lightly, but a good biographer, in my view, is one who can see both white and black and can show how a man who has this difficult pair to drive can succeed as well as fail.

"Biography," says Mr Nicolson, "is the preoccupation and solace not of certainty, but of doubt." That seems to me both profound and true. We ourselves live in an age of doubt and that is why we like to find in the lives of great men that they too have had their doubts and have nevertheless succeeded in achieving something.

We have now, I think, disentangled the essential characteristics of biography at the present time. For reasons which we have tried to explain, we demand of the historian truth purged of all passion and we believe that we find this truth in the changing aspects of a complex personality. We must go on to enquire whether it is possible to reconcile these two demands. Care for truth implies a complete apparatus of documents; is there not a danger that the personality will be buried under such a mountain? The search for historical truth is the work of the scholar; the search for the expression of a personality is rather the work of the artist; can the two things be done together? Mr Nicolson thinks not; he does not regard biography as a work of art. He thinks that there will always be a struggle between content and form and that if one must go, it had better be form. Mrs Woolf is also uneasy:

MODERN BIOGRAPHY

"The aim of biography," said Sir Sidney Lee, who had perhaps read and written more Lives than any man of his time, "is the truthful transmission of personality," and no single sentence could more neatly split up into two parts the whole problem of biography as it presents itself to us to-day. On the one hand, there is truth; on the other, there is personality. And if we think of truth as something of granite-like solidity, and of personality as something of rainbow-like intangibility and reflect that the aim of biography is to weld these two into one seamless whole, we shall admit that the problem is a stiff one and that we need not wonder if biographers have for the most part failed to solve it. For the truth of which Sir Sidney speaks, the truth which biography demands, is truth in its hardest, most obdurate form; it is truth as truth is to be found in the British Museum; it is truth out of which all vapour of falsehood has been pressed by the weight of research. Only when truth has been thus established did Sir Sidney use it in the building of his monument; and no one can be so foolish as to deny that the piles he raised of such hard facts, whether one is called Shakespeare and another King Edward the Seventh, are worthy of all our respect. For there is a virtue in truth. It has an almost mystic power. Like radium, it seems able to give off for ever and ever grains of energy, atoms of light. It stimulates the mind, which is endowed with a curious susceptibility in this direction as no fiction, however artful or highly coloured, can stimulate it. Truth being thus efficacious and supreme, we can only explain the fact that Sir Sidney's *Life of Shakespeare* is dull, and that his *Life of Edward the Seventh* is unreadable, by supposing that though both are stuffed with truth, he failed to choose those truths which transmit personality. For, in order that the light of personality may shine through, facts must be manipulated; some must be brightened; others shaded; yet, in the process, they must never lose their integrity.

It is true. It seems that insistence on truth and desire for beauty are contradictory demands. In the succeeding lectures, I propose, with your leave, to discuss "Biography considered as a work of art" and "Biography considered as a science," and I hope to be able to show you that art and science can be reconciled. A scientific book, perfectly constructed, is a work of art. A beautiful portrait is at once a portrait resembling its subject and an artistic transference of reality. It is perfectly accurate to say that truth has the solidity of stone and that personality has the lightness of a rainbow; but Rodin and the Greek sculptors before him have at times been able to infuse into marble the elusive curves and the changing lights of human flesh.

CHAPTER TWO

BIOGRAPHY AS A WORK OF ART

Chapter II

BIOGRAPHY AS A WORK OF ART

IF we could place ourselves in the position of the artist for the contemplation of our own lives, those lives would certainly give us intense aesthetic pleasure. No novelist or biographer can ever show us such fine shades of feeling as those which we could distinguish if we could contemplate our own loves, our own ambition, our own jealousy, our own happiness. But at the moment at which we ourselves display emotion, we are incapable of observation. Our emotions are too strong and leave no faculty of aesthetic criticism at our disposal. It might be easier, perhaps, to feel some aesthetic emotion from the contemplation of the lives of those around us; but nearly always we have a feeling either of affection or of antipathy towards them, and here again the strength of such feelings robs us of an attitude of detachment.

Miss Jane Harrison in her *Ancient Art and Ritual* explains this admirably:

> To see a thing, to feel a thing, as a work of art, we must, then, become for the time unpractical, must be loosed from the fear and flurry of actual

living, must become spectators. Why is this? Why can we not live and look at once? The fact that we cannot is clear. If we watch a friend drowning we do not note the exquisite curve made by his body as he falls into the water, nor the play of the sunlight on the ripples as he disappears below the surface; we should be unhuman fiends if we did. And again, why? It would do our friend no harm that we should enjoy the curves and the sunlight, provided we also threw him a rope. But the simple fact is that we *cannot* look at the curves and the sunlight because our whole being is centred on acting, on saving him; we cannot even, at the moment, fully feel our own terror and impending loss.

How, then, is a human life to give us aesthetic pleasure? First, it must be so lightly linked to our own, that, as we contemplate it, we feel no need of doing anything, no moral impulse; and to that end, perhaps the best means is that we should know it to be unreal, as when we read a novel. If we were David Copperfield and had Dora for wife, it would be a pathetic situation, of which we should not savour the beauty. In the novel, we contemplate it as a shipwreck in a picture, without feeling the need of swimming and of clutching at the nearest piece of vegetation. Certain novelists kill this aesthetic pleasure by forcing the reader to take part when they themselves set out to solve the ethical problems which their books present. But the best of them realise that this is not the artist's business. Tchekov, for instance, wrote to his friend Suvorin:

> You are confusing two things: the solution, and the correct statement, of a problem. The artist is concerned only with the second. In *Anna Karenina* no problem is solved, but the book is completely satisfying since all the problems are well stated.

But this is not the only reason why the novel appears to lighten the load of our own feelings and passions. The novel is a thing we can understand. In real life, living human beings are dangerous enigmas; it is impossible to foresee their actions; ideas seem to come to them, and then to fly away with confusing rapidity; amidst such disorder the intellect has great difficulty in finding its way. As we stand before our friends or our enemies, it is as though we stood watching a drama of infinite complexity of which we know not, of which we never shall know, the end. On the other hand, a character in a novel is built up of what the author has put into it; it is the creation of a human intellect and, as such, is accessible to a human intellect. We have no longer to deal with a divine and inexhaustible multiplicity but with a measurable and human simplicity. Of course the character may be complex (the creations of modern novelists nearly always are), but even this complexity is an ordered complexity and we can grasp it. Consider Mr Forster's *A Passage to India*: his characters are very finely shaded. He has aimed at, and succeeded in, showing us the delicate differences between the European and the Asiatic ways of thinking. Nevertheless his book is quite clear—much more so than India itself, that mysterious country with its millions of souls in which we might travel for years without understanding it. What art is concerned with is a picture of reality sufficiently far removed from us to relieve us of the desire to do something, and at the same time directed by a human will. We come back to the old Baconian definition: *Ars est homo additus naturae.*

These two qualities, then, which are essential for all aesthetic activity—an ethical neutrality and a reconstruction of nature by man—are a source of some embarrassment to us to-day as we attempt to treat of biography considered as a work of art; for they appear to debar biography, as well as history, from admission to the domain of art. In the first place, the characters of a biography are not so well adapted as those of a novel to relieve us of the necessity of acting and judging, since they have actually existed. We feel no need of judging Anna Karenina or Becky Sharp, because the people who were made to suffer by them are themselves characters in a novel. But if we read a life of Byron, we feel that there really was an actual Lady Byron, an actual Lady Caroline Lamb, and our moral impulses are stirred at the expense of our aesthetic emotions. This applies even more strongly when a statesman is concerned. When an Englishman reads a life of Gladstone or of Peel, his political and historical passions are naturally aroused and rob him of the necessary detachment. But this objection, by no means a negligible one, applies with especial force to the life either of someone still living or of someone only recently dead. So soon as the hero is dead, and dead for a sufficiently long time to relieve the reader of any feeling that what he is reading may wound a widow or a child still living, a veil of peace and security spreads itself in a remarkable way over the finished picture. Death is the greatest of the artists; by his passing, all passions are set at rest.

Perhaps biography even has an advantage over the novel. When we read the biography of a very well-known man, we know in advance what changes of fortune and what *dénouement* to expect. At first sight we might think that this might rob the book of some of its interest; but if the thing is well done, the effect is exactly the reverse. When we go to see a tragedy we know perfectly well that Caesar will in the end be murdered by Brutus, we know perfectly well that Lear will go mad; but the slow march of the drama towards these events for which we are waiting endows our emotion with that poetic grandeur which the ever-present idea of Destiny gives to Greek tragedy.

In the same way, when we read a life with the events and the end of which we are already familiar, we seem to be walking in a stretch of country which we know already, and to be reviving and completing our recollections of it. The peace of mind with which we accomplish this familiar walk is favourable to the proper aesthetic attitude[1]. Tragic beauty is, moreover, enhanced when there is a sad ending to the life. Mr Laurence Housman tells the story of a conversation in which Oscar Wilde ex-

[1] V. Alain, *Système des Beaux-Arts* (la tragédie).

plained that a life, in order to be beautiful, must end in disaster and quoted Napoleon as an example, showing that if there had been no St Helena, his life would have lost all its tragic value. One cannot help thinking that Wilde's own career owes most of its interest to the catastrophe which ended it. Sometimes the disaster is less obvious. In the case of Lord Beaconsfield the superficial observer gets an impression of marvellous success: all the ambitions of his boyhood were fulfilled in his old age. But there was an intellectual disaster, nevertheless. Measure the difference between the political vision of the Disraeli of the Young England period and the actual achievements of the aged Prime Minister and you will experience a feeling of the vanity of all things—not an ethical, but an aesthetic, feeling.

The fact, then, that the characters of a biography are real does not prevent them from being material for works of art. But there remains a second objection. We have said that the essential quality of a work of art is that it should be concerned with natural subjects reconstructed by the human spirit. *Ars est homo additus naturae.* It is essential that the spirit should have freedom of action. We know how a novelist constructs his characters: he builds them up out of feelings which act upon one another like the cog-wheels of a well-made machine; if he is a novelist of genius, the machine is so well covered in flesh that it becomes almost invisible. But it still remains a machine and the most complex hero of a novel is infinitely less complex than the most simple of human beings.

It is not so easy to understand how it is possible to construct a historical character without spoiling him. He was what he was. We cannot change him. Think of Ruskin, think of Gladstone; they were real living beings like you and me, like our friends; each of them was to those who knew them a problem, confronted by which their friends passed their lives without being able to establish any order in an over-abundant mass of observations and impressions.

What is the biographer to do? Must he try to re-create this living problem? The problem is made up of a vast accumulation of details and it would take a life-time to get through them. Ought he to group the details as in a well-designed portrait? In that case he is getting away from the real thing.

"It appears to me," says Gilbert Mauge, "that in a life which is barely ended and still fresh in the memory there is an extraordinary folly which disappears as the years roll on and that biographers fall in with this process and construct those cold, finished systems to which they give the name of Henry II or Louis XII."

To make of a man a system consistent with itself, clear, yet false, or to give up all attempts at making an intelligible system of him—such is the dilemma of the biographer.

The argument is a strong one, but it can prove equally well the impossibility of painting a landscape or a living face, since the face is too full of movement and the landscape has too much light and shade, too many different forms. Still, it is possible to paint a portrait or a landscape which may be at once a faithful image and a thing of beauty. The biographer, like the portrait-painter and the landscape-painter, must pick out the essential qualities in the whole subject which he is contemplating. By such a choice, if he can make the choice without weakening the whole, he is very precisely performing the artist's function.

The first choice he must make is that of a subject. A landscape-painter does not set himself down anywhere. He stops before a natural landscape and says, "That is well placed, or well grouped...."

Some of the great impressionists used to walk about with a frame which they tried on various aspects of the landscape before choosing the subject for their painting. So too the biographer should walk about, frame in hand, and the choice of subject is perhaps the most important thing of all for him. There are lives which have a natural beauty, which, either by chance or by some force inherent in their being, are somehow constructed like spontaneous works of art. Sometimes they display that mysterious symmetry which, when concealed under an ample clothing of flesh, endows human works with beauty. Shelley's life, for example, is a wonderful natural composition; it is grouped round two women, Harriet and afterwards Mary Godwin. Each of these women corresponds with a different stage in Shelley's ethical development and he is drawn to each by feelings which bear a fairly close resemblance to each other. The catastrophe which ends his life occurs in early youth, before the point at which the crowded and varied events of a ripe age can rob his personality of its admirable simplicity. Byron is a much more difficult hero; a novelist would have been hard put to it to construct a life as fully charged with incident as that of Byron. Nevertheless his life must also have its hidden unity; the problem is to find it.

Sir Sidney Lee writes on this question of choice that the subject of a biography "should be of a certain magnitude." One might argue that the life of every human being is interesting and that, if a biographer were capable of analysing all the thoughts which passed through the mind of an obscure beggar, such an analysis might have greater richness and beauty than a life of Caesar. Sterling, to whom Carlyle devoted two volumes, was not a well-known character and Carlyle knew it. You remember his conclusion:

> All that remains, in palpable shape, of John Sterling's activities in this world, are those two poor volumes; scattered fragments gathered from the general waste of forgotten ephemera by the piety of a friend; an inconsiderable memorial, not pretending to have achieved greatness; only disclosing mournfully, to the more observant, that a promise of greatness was there. Like other such lives, like all lives, this is a tragedy; high hopes, noble efforts; under thickening difficulties and impediments, ever-new nobleness of valiant effort;—and the result death, with conquests by no means corresponding. A life which cannot challenge the world's attention;

yet which does modestly solicit it, and perhaps on clear study will be found to reward it.

Marcel Schwob is of Carlyle's opinion:

"Biographers," he writes, "have supposed that only great men's lives could interest us. Art takes no account of such considerations. In the eyes of a painter the portrait of an unknown man by Cranach is worth as much as the portrait of Erasmus. The excellence of this latter picture is not due to the name of Erasmus. The biographer's art should contrive to set as great a price upon the life of a poor actor as upon the life of Shakespeare. It is a base instinct which makes us note with pleasure the shortened protuberance of the breast-bone in the bust of Alexander or the wisp of hair on Napoleon's forehead. The smile of Monna Lisa, of whom we know nothing (perhaps it is a man's face), is more mysterious. A grimace drawn by Hokusaï leads to still deeper contemplation. If we were practising the art in which Boswell and Aubrey excelled, we would certainly not have to describe minutely the greatest man of our age or to record the characteristics of the most famous men of the past, but to recount with the same care the individual lives of men, whether god-like, commonplace, or criminal."

A charming passage, but not wholly fair, I think. The characteristic feature of the life of an unknown man is that it leaves little trace; unless one has in mind a man of genius who has written admirable letters and has not had them published. But then, by publishing them, we bring him into the category of great writers. The novelist's choice is quite different from that of the historian. The novelist is not bound by an oath to be strictly true and to make use of nothing but documents and authentic facts. Consequently, he is entitled to analyse an unknown and commonplace character, to make him speak and think. But what can the unfortunate biographer say of a man who has left no letters, no diary, no testimonies of friends, no sign of his actions? There is only one case in which this choice may be open to him—the life-story of a character with whom he has lived. Certainly a Boswell could have "boswellised" an obscure friend of this kind, just as he boswellised Doctor Johnson, but it is extremely probable that the result would have been less interesting.

There is another argument in favour of the choice of men who have played an important part in history or in art and that is that the very expression "to play a part" is in this case something more than a metaphor. A man who exercises some lofty function (whether it be that of king or general or that special attitude which respect for his own genius imposes on a poet) reaches the point of literally "playing" a part; that is to say, his personality loses something of that obscure complexity common to all men and acquires a unity which is not wholly artificial. A great man—and often a king who is not a great man—finds himself modelled by the function he has to perform; unconsciously he aims at making his life a work of art, at becoming what the world would have him be; and so he acquires, not against his will, but in spite of himself and of whatever may be his intrinsic worth, that statuesque quality which makes him a fine model for the artist. Mr Strachey, you may be sure, did not choose Queen Victoria by accident; if Queen Victoria had not been a queen, she might have been an interesting old lady to meet; but she would not have had in her that strange and subtle element of poetry which came to her by virtue of a combination of mediocrity as a woman with the fundamental quality of a queen.

Now let us assume that the subject is chosen. Can we suggest any rules which will enable the biographer to avoid making his subject dry, and, while maintaining a scrupulous respect for scientific truth, to get somewhere near the art of the novelist? Many historians think not; some have said "No" with severe emphasis. But a Lytton Strachey certainly believes it to be possible and, like Diogenes, gives practical proof of it. Let us try to discover a few of the rules.

The first, in my view, is that of consistently following a chronological order. The ancient biographers did not follow this plan. Plutarch begins by recounting the deeds of his heroes and, at the end of the life, collects those anecdotes which illustrate character. It is an odd method, since it deprives the reader throughout the story of the interest which an intimate knowledge of the hero would add to it. Plutarch's example was followed for a very long time and it is really a very remarkable instance of imitation; for there appears to be no other reason to explain why Doctor Johnson and many Victorian biographers collected at the end of a life what they call "personal traits of character." Even the *Dictionary of National Biography*, well constructed and remarkable as it is from other points of view, accepts, as an unchangeable rule, the order: Facts first, Character afterwards.

It seems to me extremely difficult to interest a reader in facts which are not presented in their normal order. The romantic interest of a life springs from just that anticipation of the future, from that finding of ourselves on the brink of the abyss which is To-morrow, without any conception of what we shall find there. Even when the man is famous and the reader knows perfectly well that the hero is destined to become a great general or a great poet in the end, it seems rather absurd to tell him so in the first sentence of the book. Why begin a biography as Forster begins that of Dickens? "Charles Dickens, the most popular novelist of this country and one of the greatest humorists which England has produced, was born at Portsea on Friday, 7 February 1812."

No; no popular novelist or great humorist was ever born. There was born on 7 February 1812 a little baby, just as a little baby was born on Wellington's, or on Shakespeare's, birthday.

Are we then to pretend ignorance of what we know perfectly well? Are we to pretend, at the beginning of a life of a great general, that we have forgotten the whole of his career? Strictly speaking, I think we are. It is an artifice, perhaps, but the word "artifice" contains the word "art." The author of a tragedy does not suggest to us, in his first few lines, what the *dénouement* is to be. The author of a biography realises, of course, that the reader knows the *dénouement*; but it is not for him to advertise it on the first page. He must begin simply, with no desire to shine, but with the one object of placing his reader in an atmosphere which will facilitate his understanding of the first feelings of the hero in his youth.

Perhaps we may feel the need for chronological sequence more keenly than the old biographers because we do not believe, as they did, in the existence of unchangeable characters. We accept the evolution of the individual spirit just as we accept the evolution of the race. We believe that character develops but slowly, by contact with human beings and with events. A character always consistent with itself at every moment of the life of the hero is for us an intellectual abstraction; it is not a reality. Our point of view is that put by Miss Lowell at the beginning of her biography of Keats:

> My object has been to make the reader feel as though he were living with Keats, subject to the same influences that surrounded him, moving in his

circle, watching the advent of poems as from day to day they sprang into being.

It is difficult to make biography a work of art if the influence of events and people on the hero's character is not shown progressively and as they appeared to him. For instance, in a biography of Byron, it would not, in my view, be allowable to present a portrait of Shelley as he was before the moment when Byron first knew him, and it is desirable that the portrait should be as close as possible to what Shelley was in Byron's eyes at that moment.

One of the fundamental facts of life is the slow process of change in the minds of each one of us and in the characters of our friends. One whom we have regarded as perfect suddenly appears to us as fallible. This happened with Shelley and Godwin; it happened with John Manners and Disraeli. It is not the business of the biographer to anticipate the discoveries of his hero. Nothing tends more to destroy the sense of movement than such a sentence as: "Though his impression had been favourable, he was afterwards to discover...." Mr Forster, following the French philosopher Alain, explained in his lectures on the novel last year that this question of the point of view is of the first importance in the construction of a novel. Three solutions are possible: either to see everything through the hero's eyes; or to see the action through the eyes of each one of the characters in turn; or to take the point of view of a creator and so make the action dominated by the novelist himself.

For biography I frankly prefer the first method, though I do not forget the necessity of occasionally taking up such a position at an infinite distance, in order to show how the hero is reflected in the faulty mirrors represented by the people who surround him.

In particular, great historical events bound up with the life of a statesman ought not to be treated in a biography as they are treated in a history. If a man is writing a life of Napoleon, his real subject is the spiritual and emotional development of Napoleon; history should be seen only in the background and to such a degree as may be necessary for the understanding of this development, and the biographer must try to give it something of the appearance which it had in the emperor's eyes. Take a simple instance like the battle of Austerlitz. In a well-written history it may, it ought, to be described in all its aspects; in a biography of Napoleon it should be the battle which Napoleon conceived and saw. A good example of this is the battle of Waterloo, as seen by Fabrice at the beginning of *La Chartreuse de Parme*.

Edmund Gosse has put the point very well:

> Broad views are entirely out of place in biography; and there is no greater literary mistake than to attempt what is called the *Life and Times* of a man. History deals with fragments of the vast roll of events; it must always begin abruptly and close in the middle of affairs; it must altogether deal, impartially, with a vast number of persons. Biography is a study sharply defined by two definite events: birth and death. It fills the canvas with one figure, and other characters, however great in themselves, must always be subsidiary to the central hero.

Another characteristic quality of a work of art is the choice of details. A scholar, as such, may accumulate an enormous number of facts on any subject and display them all without selection. But, I believe that, in fact, a great scholar makes his selection from the beginning and, by tracing certain general lines, produces an artist's work. The biographer who is also an artist must, above all things, relieve his reader of the burden of useless material.

It is his duty to read everything himself, because, if he does not, he risks missing an important detail or accepting a fact as authentic which other documents prove to be false; but, once his scaffolding is firm and his house built, he pulls down the scaffolding and is at pains to present to the reader the completed house and nothing more.

Biography, in my view, does not consist in telling all one knows—for in that case the most trifling book would be as long as life itself—but in taking stock of one's knowledge and of choosing what is essential. It goes without saying that in making this choice, the biographer often finds himself tempted to emphasise that particular aspect of a character which he knows and loves best. From this it sometimes comes about that the hero is distorted by the artist-biographer. But is less distortion wrought by the bad arrangement of documents, by the absence of "values" (in the painter's sense), in the work of the heavy-handed biographer who produces a dull portrait of a striking countenance?

In this discarding of the useless, the biographer must not lose sight of the fact that the smallest details are often the most interesting. Everything that can give us an idea of what the man actually looked like, the tone of his voice, the style of his conversation, is essential. The part played by the body in helping to form our ideas of the character of our acquaintances should always be borne in mind. For us a man primarily consists of a certain physical aspect, a certain look, familiar gestures, a voice, a smile, a series of habitual expressions; all these must be made to live again for us in the man who is presented through the medium of a book. It is the historian's most difficult task. The personality transmitted through documents is above all things an abstract personality, hardly known except by his actions towards his fellow-men. If he is not capable of making us see a being of flesh and blood behind the clouds of papers and speeches and actions, he is lost.

"Historical science," says Marcel Schwob, "leaves us in uncertainty about individual people. It merely shows us their points of contact with general events. It tells us that Napoleon was ill on the day of Waterloo, that we must attribute Newton's immense intellectual activity to the absolute continence of his personal temperament, that Alexander was drunk when he killed Clitus and that Louis XIV's ulcer may have been the cause of certain of his decisions. Pascal argues about Cleopatra's nose—

what would have happened if it had been shorter?—and about the grain of sand in Cromwell's bladder. All these individual facts matter only because they have modified events or because they might have altered the order of events. They are actual, or potential, causes. They must be left to scholars.

"Art is the exact opposite of general ideas. It describes only what is individual and desires only what is unique. It does not classify; it takes things out of their classes. So far as we are concerned, our general ideas may be like those which obtain in the planet Mars, and three lines which cut each other must make a triangle in any part of the universe. But consider a leaf of a tree, with its wayward system of colours varying with sun and shade, the swelling produced on it by a single raindrop, the tiny hole made by an insect, the silvery track of a little snail, the first fatal gilding which is the sign of autumn; try to find a leaf exactly like it in all the great forests of the earth; I defy you to find it. There is no science of the teguments of a leaflet, of the filaments of a cell, of the curvature of a vein, of the violence of a habit, of the idiosyncrasies of a character. That a man had a twisted nose, or one eye higher than the other, or knotty arm-joints; that he was accustomed to eat a *blanc de poulet* at a particular hour, that he preferred Malvoisie to Château Margaux—these are things without parallel in the world. Thales might have said 'Gnothi seauton' just as well as Socrates, but he would not have rubbed his leg in prison in the same way before drinking the hemlock. Great men's ideas are the common heritage of humanity; their only individual possessions are their oddities. The book which should describe a man in all his inconsistencies would be a work of art like a Japanese print, displaying a series of pictures of a tiny caterpillar seen once at one particular hour of the day."

The strength of Aubrey and of Boswell lies exactly in their gusto for such details. Boswell has given us a perfect idea of what Johnson's tone of voice may have been. Marcel Schwob rejoices in the fact that Diogenes Laertius

informs us that Aristotle carried on his stomach a leather purse full of warm oil and that after his death a number of earthenware jars were found in his house. We shall never know what Aristotle did with all these bits of pottery; and the mystery is as delightful as the mystery in which Boswell leaves us in the matter of the use Johnson made of the dried orange-peel which he was in the habit of keeping in his pockets.

Aubrey tells us that Spenser was a little man, that he wore his hair short with a little collar and cuffs; that Erasmus disliked fish and that none of Bacon's servants dared appear before him without boots of Spanish leather, "for he would smell the neates-leather, which offended him." It is impossible to understand the 18th Brumaire unless one knows that on that day Napoleon had pimples and had scratched himself—hence his gory face and the mistake of the grenadiers.

There is nothing more delightful in the writing of a biography than the pursuit of vivid details like these across the pages of memoirs and letters. Sometimes one may read hundreds of pages without finding anything but general ideas—and those false ideas. Then, quite suddenly, in the by-way of a phrase there appears a sign of life and the faithful reader stops and grasps it. What a joy, for instance, to discover that d'Orsay used to laugh loudly when he said "Ha, ha," and gripped his friends' hands too vigorously. Mr Strachey plays this game admirably: he knows that the little Victoria used, in her childhood, to be taught by the Baroness de Späth to make little cardboard boxes trimmed with gold paper and painted flowers. He notes that Victoria's journal has the appearance of being written by a child, but that her letters seem to be the work of a child corrected by a governess. He brings before our eyes an evening party at Windsor—the circle of people at the round table, the albums of the queen's sketches, with the Prince playing his interminable games of chess with three of his gentlemen-in-waiting. No one was ever more conscious of the importance of authentic detail than the hero of the best of all biographies, Dr Johnson himself:

> The business of a biographer is often to pass slightly over those performances and incidents which produce vulgar greatness, to lead the thoughts into domestick privacies, and display the minute details of daily life, where exterior appendages are cast aside, and men excel each other only by prudence and by virtue....
>
> There are many invisible circumstances which... are more important than publick occurrences. Thus Sallust, the great master of nature, has not forgot, in his account of Cataline, to remark that *his walk was now quick, and again slow*, as an indication of a mind revolving something with violent commotion.
>
> Thus the story of Melanchthon affords a striking lecture on the value of time, by informing us, that when he made an appointment, he expected not only the hour, but the minute to be fixed, that the day might not run out in the idleness of suspense: and all the plans and enterprizes of De Witt are now of

less importance to the world, than that part of his personal character, which represents him as *careful of his health, and negligent of his life.*

But biography has often been allotted to writers who seem very little acquainted with the nature of their task.... They rarely afford any other account than might be collected from publick papers, but imagine themselves writing a life when they exhibit a chronological series of actions or preferments; and so little regard the manners or behaviour of their heroes, that more knowledge may be gained of a man's real character, by a short conversation with one of his servants, than from a formal and studied narrative, begun with his pedigree, and ended with his funeral.

From this passage it is clear that Johnson had a vision of what a certain type of biography might be, the type which was later to be exemplified by Mr Strachey. Moreover, as one reads Johnson's own *Lives of the Poets*, one is struck by the Stracheyesque touch to be found in many of them. In fact, one has but to entitle one half of the work *Eminent Jacobeans* and the other *Eminent Augustans* to make it a wholly modern book. Milton undergoes at Johnson's hands a much severer treatment than Cardinal Manning at Mr Strachey's: "Milton soon determined to repudiate her for disobedience; and, being one of those who could easily find arguments to justify inclination, published (in 1644) *The Doctrine and Discipline of Divorce.*" Johnson is full of touches of this kind.

Must I confess that, as a work of art, I prefer *Eminent Victorians*? Johnson's moral judgments crop up with a vigour which is entertaining but at the same time spoils, or at least displaces, the effect. "The brutality of his invective," he says again of Milton, "was equalled only by the vulgarity of his flattery." This is, in my view, a form of judgment too heavy to be delivered by the biographer on the subject of a biography. Objectivity and detachment are the supreme aesthetic virtues. Like the novelist, the biographer must "expose" and not "impose." A great life well told always carries a suggestion of a philosophy of life, but it gains nothing by an expression of that philosophy.

Can a biography have a poetic value? I think it can. Poetry, in the wide sense, I conceive to be a transmutation of nature into some beautiful form, made intelligible by the introduction of rhythm. In poetry, in the stricter sense, this rhythm is established by the verse-form or by rhyme; in music, by the motif; in a book by the recurrence, at more or less distant intervals, of the essential motifs of the work.

A human life is always made up of a number of such motifs; when you study one of them, it will soon begin to impress itself upon you with a remarkable force. In Shelley's life the water motif dominates the whole symphony. It is by the banks of a river that we first find him dreaming in his youth at Eton; it is on a stream that he afterwards launches his fragile and symbolical paper boats; then his life is spent in ships; his first wife, Harriet, dies of drowning and the vision of a watery death haunts the reader for a long time before the actual event, as though Destiny had been leading Shelley from childhood towards the bay of Spezzia.

In Disraeli's life there is a flower motif, which sometimes takes the form of a pot of geraniums sent by his sister, sometimes of the queen's primroses; there is an Eastern motif, clear and piercing, which sounds with a blare of trumpets in youth, but gradually the brazen sounds are softened and, as death approaches, are nothing but a distant echo muffled by the strains of English violins; and there is the antagonistic rain motif, that terrible English rain which sets out to extinguish the over-brilliant

Eastern flame and succeeds; the rain which at the beginning puts to flight the muddy knights of the Eglinton tournament, the rain which submerges Peel and robs the Hughenden peacocks of their feathers; the rain which in the end carries off the sun-kissed wizard himself.

Of this magnificent poetry of life Mr Strachey has made himself a master, and I know few finer passages than those last pages of *Queen Victoria*, in which he shows us all the motifs of the queen's life passing through her dying consciousness:

The spring woods at Osborne, so full of primroses for Lord Beaconsfield...Lord Palmerston's queer clothes and high demeanour, and Albert's face under the green lamp, and Albert's first stag at Balmoral, and Albert in his blue and silver uniform, and the Baron coming in through a doorway, and Lord M. dreaming at Windsor with the rooks cawing in the elm-trees, and the Archbishop of Canterbury on his knees in the dawn, and the old king's turkey-cock ejaculations, and Uncle Leopold's soft voice at Claremont, and Lehzen with the globes, and her mother's feathers sweeping down towards her, and a great old repeater-watch of her father's in its tortoise-shell case, and a yellow rug, and some friendly flounces of sprigged muslin, and the trees and the grass at Kensington.

It is a page that makes one think of the funeral march of Siegfried, or of the motifs of the Tetralogy as they return shrouded in crêpe at the end of the *Twilight of the Gods*. The mind savours a poetic melancholy at this rapid survey of the past. We gather up in one poor bunch the rare blooms which have given a life its perfume, and we offer them to the Fates which have been fulfilled. It is the last refrain of a dying song, the last stanza of a consummated poem. Here the biographer is on a level with the great musician and the great poet.

CHAPTER THREE

BIOGRAPHY CONSIDERED AS A SCIENCE

Chapter III

BIOGRAPHY CONSIDERED AS A SCIENCE

NO two views of history could be more different than those of Froude and of Mr Nicolson. Froude does not believe in historical truth. He quotes Talleyrand's remark with approval: "There is nothing which can so easily be arranged as facts," and says himself, "The most perfect history of England is to be found, in my opinion, in Shakespeare's historical plays." In another passage he imagines himself, in company with other historians, being arraigned before a tribunal for the examination of his work; the judges have a magical liquid which has the power of obliterating everything that is false in his books; page after page, chapter after chapter disappears, leaving just a judgment here and there and generally one which he formed with the least care, one which his critics had most violently attacked.

But Mr Harold Nicolson courageously takes a stand in opposition to Froude:

I would suggest, in the first place, that the scientific interest in biography is hostile to, and will in the end prove destructive of the literary interest. The former will insist not only on the facts, but on all the facts. The scientific interest, as it develops, will become insatiable; no synthetic power, no genius for representation, will be able to keep the pace. I foresee, therefore, a divergence between the two interests. Scientific biography will become specialised and technical. There will be biographies in which development will be traced in all its intricacy and in a manner comprehensible only to the experts; there will be biographies examining the influence of heredity—biographies founded on Galton, on Lombroso, on Havelock Ellis, on Freud; there will be medical biographies—studies of the influence on character of the endocrine glands, studies of internal secretions; there will be sociological biographies, aesthetic biographies, philosophical biographies. These will doubtless be interesting and instructive, but the emphasis which will be thrown on the analytical or scientific aspect will inevitably lessen the literary effort applied to their composition. The more that biography becomes a branch of science, the less will it become a branch of literature.

Our question to-day is this: Is there, in biography, a scientific truth? And it seems to me that the question naturally divides itself into two: first, is it possible to know the truth about a man?

secondly, to what extent can we discover the truth about a time, or a period, in recording the history of a man?

What material is at our disposal for the discovery of the truth about a man? First of all, there are the works of those who have previously written about him. These, of course, must be read with great care but, whenever they are accessible, we must turn preferably to original documents. Nothing is an adequate substitute for the personal impression to be obtained from direct contact with a man's letters or diary. At the hands of those who have already used them they have undergone a change. It is the same in actual life: we meet ten witnesses who give their description of some particular man; each of them has his own opinion about him; those who have never seen him have invented a legend about him; those who have met him remember nothing but an anecdote and how the man looked for a particular moment—an appearance which they identify with the whole man. When we afterwards find ourselves face to face with the real man, when we discover the man himself, we are completely astonished to see how little the real Poincaré, for instance, resembles the Poincaré of legend. We expected a lawyer's face, severe, geometrical; instead, we find gentle eyes and an almost ingenuous expression.

The same applies to the past. Here contact is only possible through the medium of the written word and it is, in consequence, imperfect. Nevertheless, the actual words written by the man himself have a particular tone, a particular shade of significance, which no paraphrase can preserve. I remember my surprise when I read Byron's Ravenna journal for the first time. There I grasped what no biography had made me see before—Byron in front of his fire:

> Stayed at home all the morning—looked at the fire—wondered when the post would come.... Wrote five letters in about half an hour, short and savage....Hear the carriage—order pistols and great coat, as usual—necessary articles. Weather cold—carriage open, and inhabitants somewhat savage—...highly inflamed by politics. Fine fellows though, good materials for a nation....Clock strikes—going out to make love. Somewhat perilous, but not disagreeable.
>
> Thought of the state of women under the ancient Greeks—convenient enough. Present state a rem-

nant of the barbarism of the chivalry and feudal ages—artificial and unnatural. They ought to mind home—and be well fed and clothed—but not mixed in society. Well educated, too, in religion—but to read neither poetry nor politics—nothing but books of piety and cookery. Music, drawing, dancing—also a little gardening and ploughing now and then. I have seen them mending the roads in Epirus with great success. Why not, as well as hay-making and milking?

Came home...and played with my mastiff,—gave him his supper....The crow is lame of a leg—wonder how it happened—some fool trod upon his toe, I suppose. The falcon pretty brisk—the cats large and noisy,—the monkeys I have not looked to since the cold weather, as they suffer by being brought up. Horses must be gay—get a ride as soon as weather serves. Deuced muggy still—an Italian winter is a sad thing, but all the other seasons are charming.

What is the reason that I have been, all my lifetime, more or less *ennuyé*? And that, if anything, I am rather less so now than I was at twenty, as far as my recollection serves? I do not know how to answer this, but presume that it is constitutional.... Temperance and exercise, which I have practised at times...made little or no difference. Violent passions did;—when under their immediate influence—it is odd, but—I was in agitated, but not in depressed, spirits....Swimming also raises my spirits, but in general they are low and get daily lower. That is *hopeless*; for I do not think that I am so much *ennuyé* as I was at nineteen. The proof is, that then I must game, or drink, or be in motion of some kind, or I was miserable. At present I can mope in quietness.

I would willingly give the lives of Byron by Moore and Elze and Edgcumbe and all the rest, even Trelawny, for a few such pages of the diary.

Yes, this particular note given forth by every human soul, whose pure echo is so delightful to the ear, comes from original documents and it is useless to seek for it anywhere else. But to what degree do these original documents themselves convey the truth to us? Few such documents are generally available; not many men keep a diary and most modern men write but few letters. Of those who have kept a diary, it is a rare thing to find one who has kept it all his life. The diary stands for exceptional moments in a life and we shall be sorely tempted to see in it a representation of the whole of a life. Such a view is all the more misleading when the notion of keeping a diary has occurred only at times of crisis, with the result that we neglect the normal and habitual aspect of our subject.

But further, even if we confine our attention to those periods for which we have a diary, how are we to be sure that the diary exactly represented the mind of the man who wrote it? Certain diaries are written with an eye to posterity; the author adopts a definite attitude in his writing, and complacently anticipates the effect which his attitude will produce upon the reader. Even when the diary is honestly not intended to be read, the writer is very often posing to himself. He has visualised a certain attitude, he finds it pleasing, and he experiences an aesthetic pleasure in exaggerating it. Every memorialist is an author, whether he wishes it or not; the *ego* which he has established on his writing-paper becomes a separate entity; he contemplates it at a distance, sometimes with horror, sometimes with admiration, but in both cases with an aesthetic detachment which gives many diaries a high literary value, but at the same time completely destroys their value as psychological documents. The most favourable instance is that of a man like Pepys, who is primarily a recorder of facts and is not a victim of the modern curse of introspection. Of course, a clever psychologist can extract some profit even from a diary which is falsified for the reasons we have just given by interpreting it in the light of other documents; but it is a very delicate task which depends upon a sense of artistic perception much more than upon scientific method.

I should say much the same about correspondence and about conversations reported by witnesses. Of course, they are all important documents, but here again only to be properly valued by being interpreted by a creative imagination. They are almost always contradictory; all men and women present very different appearances of themselves to other people. The Shelley who writes to Godwin is a different creature from the Shelley who writes to Miss Hitchener or to Hogg. The Byron who writes to Lady Melbourne is a cynic; the Byron who talks with Lady Blessington is almost a sentimentalist. It is true that the correspondence with Lady Melbourne does not belong to the same year as the conversations with Lady Blessington and, of course, time plays a part in this psychological change, but there is also a fact of more general significance and one with which we are all familiar; it is that, by an involuntary mimicry, we model ourselves upon what the other person expects of us. Byron writes on the fly-leaf of a copy of *Corinne* belonging to the Countess Guiccioli:

I feel I exist here, and I feel that I shall exist hereafter—to *what* purpose you will decide; my destiny rests with you....I love you and you love me,—at least you *say so*, and *act* as if you *did* so, which last is a great consolation in all events. But *I* more than love you and cannot cease to love you.

And in the same week, referring to Teresa Guiccioli, he writes to Hobhouse:

I can't say I don't feel the degradation. Better be an unskilful planter, an awkward settler—better be a hunter, or anything, than a flatterer of fiddlers and fan-carrier of a woman....And now I am a *cavalier servant*—by the Holy! it is a strange sensation.

Musset, the French counterpart of Byron, at the very time when he was writing to George Sand—

Posterity will recall our names as those of such immortal lovers as have nothing in the world but each other, such lovers as Romeo and Juliet or Héloïse and Abélard...

—was recording feelings which led him immediately afterwards to remark:

While I was composing my poems, she was scribbling over reams of paper....This tête-à-tête every day with a woman older than myself, a face growing always more and more serious in front of me—all this revolted the spirit of youth within me and filled me with bitter regret for my former liberty....

In the volatile personality of a Byron or a Musset, such impressions are, no doubt, perfectly sincere and illustrate the varying moods of the men themselves. But, in other instances, a letter may be the work of a hypocrite and express nothing at all of the writer's true feelings. This is the case with the excellent Godwin: if we read Godwin's letters to Shelley, or his letters to Edward Bulwer Lytton, without connecting them with what we know of Godwin's life and habits, he appears to us as a saint—which is very far from the truth. Thus all these personal documents, precious though they may be, are valuable only in so far as they are put face to face with each other and with the complete picture of the man's personality. Such a process, when it is feasible, reveals to us weaknesses, falsehoods, and mistakes and throws a marvellously bright light upon our hero; but, once again, it is the work of the artist rather than of the scholar.

When we are dealing with a writer, there is one extremely tempting document—his written work;

and the first tendency of every biographer is to interpret the work in an autobiographical sense. It is quite natural. Obviously no writer knows any other soul so well as he knows his own; when he wants to portray men, he utilises fragments of his own character. As Mr Forster explained to you last year, the characters of a novel are masses of words which represent certain qualities of the author himself:

> The novelist, unlike many of his colleagues, makes up a number of word-masses roughly describing himself (roughly: niceties shall come later), gives them names and sex, assigns them plausible gestures, and causes them to speak by the use of inverted commas, and perhaps to behave consistently. These word-masses are his characters.

Thus it seems possible, and often easy, to discover the man underneath his characters. We may construct a Dickens according to *David Copperfield*, or a Meredith according to *Evan Harrington*, or a Stendhal according to Fabrice and Julien, or Balzac's childhood according to that of Felix de Vandenesse. This may have an air of truth, but it is extremely dangerous. Thomas Hardy, turning the pages of a book about himself, said to a visitor:

Why are people not more careful in deducing biographical and semi-biographical facts from an author's books? People used to say that David Copperfield was Dickens. He was not.... Mr Hedgcock is continually drawing on the novels for descriptions of my character. His dissection would not be in good taste while I am still alive, even if it were true. But it is based chiefly on characters and incidents in the novels that are pure invention.... Mr Hedgcock's besetting fault of getting behind the novels of the writer leads to numerous inaccuracies. Thus he says that I was brought up to speak the local dialect. I did not speak it. I knew it, but it was not spoken at home. My mother only used it when speaking to the cottagers, and my father when speaking to his workmen. The account of my education is full of errors. It is stated that I was educated at an elementary school and was deprived of a classical training. I was only at an elementary school for a year or two, till I was ten, and I learnt Latin at school from my twelfth year. Again, he says I learnt the classics by correspondence—deluded by his false identification of me with Smith in *A Pair of Blue Eyes*. The same source of error leads to the ascription to myself of the disgust felt for architecture by a character in *Desperate Remedies*.... When he comes to Smith, he makes some of his worst mistakes—one unwarranted assumption after another. The description of his appearance is not at all like what I was. His father was not at all like mine. He was a Cornishman and a journey-man. Smith himself was a Weymouth man—as far as he was based on any real person, which he was not much. On one page he identifies me with Springrove, and another with Clym....

Anyone who has written a novel himself, will well understand Thomas Hardy. A character in a novel is built up not of the whole of the author's personality, but often of a very tiny fragment of his *ego*. From the fact that Proust has written some admirable pages on jealousy I should hesitate to infer that Proust was a jealous man, especially towards the end of his life. To have experienced an emotion strongly for a few days, or even a few minutes, is quite enough to enable a man to describe it. Often the mere description is enough to prevent him feeling it again; in such a case the man's work is a means of deliverance. Possibly—I know nothing of this; it is pure hypothesis—possibly it might be true to say: Meredith pilloried the egoist because he was himself an egoist, and Meredith ceased to be an egoist because he had written *The Egoist*.

Furthermore, in creating a character in a novel an author does not concentrate his attention upon himself and find everything there that he wants; a novelist is a man who knows something of others, who finds his way about the world. Even if he has discovered his hero's first pattern in himself, he finds in others a countless number of qualities which will feed and vitalise this central character. If we biographers accept this central character as the exact representation of the author, we shall expose ourselves to serious error.

Further, it often happens that a writer constructs his work in order to gain for himself, in a world of the imagination, what actual life has denied him—Dickens, for example, in the marriage of David and Agnes. In this case the novel is not autobiographical; it is exactly the reverse and it is only by quite an indirect approach that we can utilise it as documentary material. What happens in fact is that an author moulds his work less than the work moulds him; and, in a certain sense, he becomes its slave. The *Childe Harold* humour did exist for Byron, but it was a transient humour. Yet the public will not have it that its favourite author does not resemble his creation; it exerts a gentle, but powerful, pressure to force the author into the mould of the character he has created; and when the character is popular, alluring and attractive to women, the author gives way. The biographer must be on the alert and seek to explain Byron by *Childe Harold* rather than *Childe Harold* by Byron.

French literary historians have recently had an excellent example of the errors into which they may be led by this method, even in what appeared to be the clearest case. Everyone believed that Balzac had been inspired to write *Le Lys dans la vallée* by his first mistress, Mme de Berny. A book recently published by M. Charles Léger, entitled *Balzac mis à nu*, has brought new documents to light and shows that Balzac's original in this particular story was the Countess Guidoboni-Visconti. At the very moment when Balzac was writing to a foreigner, Mme Hanska, "Oh, you don't know what three years of chastity means!" everyone in Paris knew about his liaison with Mme Guidoboni-Visconti, by whom he had a son in 1836[1].

I believe, however (though I may be wrong), that there is one case in which there is no great danger in assuming that a work has been in large measure inspired by actual life—I mean when every one of an author's works contains the same character under

[1] This, too, will some day cease to be true.

a different name. In Stendhal's works it is very striking how Fabrice, Julien Sorel and Lucien Leuwen are exactly the same man—a man who is not what Stendhal was, but is very clearly what Stendhal would have liked to be. These characters have no autobiographical, but a considerable expository, value. It is the same when, in Disraeli's first two novels, *Vivian Grey* and *Contarini Fleming*, we find in both heroes the same period of youth, the same school fight described in almost identical terms; here, I think (though I would shrink from dogmatising) that we have a right to infer that we are dealing with a real obsession and that the narrative would not be so vivid if it were not real. I should say as much about the childhood of Dickens, and with still more confidence, for there we have the testimony of John Forster, who drew from Dickens an avowal of the autobiographical character of *David Copperfield*, whatever Thomas Hardy may say of it. We may add that we are certainly more justified in believing in the autobiographical quality of novels written in early youth than in that of novels written at a riper age. A young man of twenty has great difficulty in not writing of himself; even when he is writing a novel, he is a lyrical poet; in spite of himself his real sentiments burst out; the critical function which will come into active play in the matured writer and will hinder the expression of sentiments, on the ground that they will be considered ridiculous or dangerous or commonplace, is as yet absent from the young man's mind. But you see how few cases there are in which it is permissible to draw inferences from a man's work and even in such cases what serious errors such inferences may produce.

What is there still left that may be considered as an element in the discovery of truth? There is one document of high value—the memoirs of contemporaries. It is amongst them that we must hunt for those tiny, infinitely precious pictures which reveal to us what our hero was in the eyes of the man who actually met him. When the witness is intelligent, when he has the gift of sight, then he provides us with the most valuable form of document. Where shall we get a more revealing picture of Louis Philippe than in the short note made by Victor Hugo immediately after a visit he paid to the king? What better portrait of Disraeli in his old age could we have than that recorded after a visit to him by Mr Hyndman in his *Record of an Adventurous Life*?

But here again we must weigh and compare impressions, since those received, by contemporaries, of the same man may be very different. Always we are driven back to the same idea: finding no one of the elements of a biographical truth to be strictly scientific, we are compelled to have recourse to a kind of psychological imaginativeness, and, in many instances, the truth about a particular event is impossible to determine. I will give you two examples. You know the story of the letter sent by Shelley to Byron to clear himself of the accusations of Elise, the chamber-maid; you know that this letter, which was meant to be passed on to the Hoppners, was found amongst Byron's papers after his death. There are two possible solutions: (1) Byron never sent the letter, (2) Byron sent the letter which was returned to him by the Hoppners. On the first hypothesis, Byron behaved badly; on the second, he did precisely what he ought to have done. What is the truth? Pirandello alone could tell us: *Cosi è se vi pare.*

Here is another example of the same kind: the letter from Disraeli to Peel, which Disraeli denied in the House of Commons. Had he forgotten its existence at the time when he was speaking? In that case he is innocent. Had he not forgotten it? In that case he is not only a liar but a clumsy fool, since there was every reason to believe that Peel would have kept a letter of that kind. The truth is that the nearer we press towards actual facts, the more clearly we see that biography cannot be treated like physics and chemistry. In all the sciences of which the object is to investigate the relations between material substances experiment is possible, because we can control the experience; if we have not clearly observed what happens when sodium and water are brought together, we have simply to begin again and watch more closely the second time. But the proper function of biography is to deal with the individual and the instantaneous.

There was a minute, a second, at which Byron made up his mind about the letter to the Hoppners; at that moment he made a movement either of throwing it into a drawer, or of putting it into an envelope addressed to them. It was a moment which we can never recover, a unique experience which we can never behold again; hence the impossibility of our employing what is the essence of the scientific method.

"The historian's trade," writes Mme Pailleron,

"is a terrible trade. How can one practise it with any security? In the first place, what do we know? Are you relying upon oral tradition? Who, amongst those that transmit it, is going to inspire you with confidence? Unless you are convinced of the soundness of their memories, of their impartiality and, I may add, of their lack of imagination, you are running great risks. Are you consulting other researchers? Mind you verify their texts. Are you using family papers, letters, documents which can scarcely be false? Are you building up your own opinion on the basis of them, are you taking sides? But see, some time afterwards there come other documents, containing fresh revelations. You thought your hero an honest man; so he was in his youth, but he ended at the galleys. You have described a man as a bronzed, upright figure and you find that he had a hump on his back. A faithful friend? You thought so. And so he was at the moment you chose to portray him; the next day, behold, he was a traitor. Your book crashes to the ground. You have assured your reader that such and such a man was faithful in love. Have you not held his letters in your hands? 'I am alone,' he wrote, 'I see no women, I live in a cell. What a gloomy life, what misery!' Nonsense! he suffers no misery, so far from his being alone, you shortly learn that he had become, at that hour precisely, the father of a fine boy...furthermore, that he corresponds with two ladies who, of their charity, pay visits to the hermit from time to time.

"Hence the discouragement of the historian, the uncertainty and disillusionment of the researcher, who cannot even place any confidence in death and say to himself: 'That man has lain in his grave for a century; I have no surprises to fear.' Yes, there are always surprises, as many in death as in life and all the more cruel because they have had longer to wait."

Consider the case of Carlyle and his wife. He was first described by the historian Froude, and Froude's thesis was that Jane Carlyle was a sensitive, unhappy, misunderstood woman compelled by Carlyle's selfishness and dyspepsia to lead a servant's life, only to be deceived as soon as fame brought her husband the opportunity of friendship with other ladies. But now read Miss Drew's recent book on Jane Carlyle. Her thesis is exactly opposite:

It is impossible not to admire Carlyle's unfailing gentleness and loyalty to her in the face of the often petty and querulous complaints she makes to him of his shortcomings, or what she considers are his shortcomings. She is often voluble, aggressive and resentful for no just cause whatever. She has a very nasty tongue when she is on edge; and no wonder Carlyle was hurt when she dismisses a long letter he has written her, by saying 'it will read charmingly in your biography.'...Of course she is always sorry after she has been unkind to him, but he *never* loses patience with her, assuring her that he is glad she makes her "bits of complaints" freely to him, as he can understand and sympathise with her in everything she has to suffer, if only she will trust him and believe in his love....But she suffered all her life from a love of dramatising herself....It was really perhaps the result of a craving for creative power, and the fact that she just fell short of any real creative power. She had a strong dash of the artistic temperament without any ability to produce art, and it was that which drove her to pose continually in some dramatic rôle.

Here are two entirely different theses. Well, both are supported by extracts from letters, all correctly quoted, all convincing. To a certain extent the different verdicts are due to the fact that Froude was a man and loved his heroine, whilst Miss Drew is a woman and has naturally more sympathy with Carlyle. But, for one reason or another, we are driven back always to the same conclusion: it is impossible, in history, to arrive at scientific truth.

Of course I am well aware that we shall be told: "You will have medical biographies; you will have studies of internal secretions; you will have biographies founded upon Freud." Very well, but will they be interesting? And, in the first place, how are we going to get them? What do we know about the medical history of the great men of the past? What will be known in the future about the medical history of men living to-day? Who is engaged at the present moment in preserving notes on the internal secretions of Einstein? Who is investigating the endocrine glands of Paul Valéry? Who is keeping a record of Bertrand Russell's dreams, so that the Freudian biographers may interpret them at a later date? And if all these points are not recorded even during the life of the individual, they too are unique, irreversible, irrecoverable. Even assuming that the scientific study of man makes great progress, that we develop the habit of attaching to great men a very complete dossier of records from the physico-chemical or biological points of view, how are we to foresee that a man is going to be great? Who is to choose the subjects for observation at a youthful stage? Even if you assume that we shall reach the stage of establishing a vast medical bureaucracy and that each one of us will have a formidable dossier filed in some ministry of hygiene, can you seriously believe that what we shall find in those files will be the truth about a man?

Think of your own life. Imagine that from the Elysian Fields you are privileged to contemplate the labours of your biographer. Would you be pleased to see him poring over dreams and statistics? "But that is not myself," you would say, "those things were of no interest except to my doctor." Would you like to see him turning over the pages of your books and deducing from them that you had done things quite foreign to your nature? "That is not myself," you would say, "that is the work of my imagination." Would it please you to see him collecting phrases from your letters? "That!" you would say, "Why, but I never thought a word of it even at the moment when I was writing it!" Then he indiscreetly opens your diary, and you would pityingly murmur: "Why bother with that fortnight during which I passed through a crisis of mad folly?"

The truth about your own life? Why, you would be very hard put to it to describe it yourself. It is a confused medley of actions, thoughts, and feelings, very often contradictory, yet possessing a certain unity which is, as it were, a sort of musical tone. Your life is written in C minor or in A major. You feel it, but you would have great difficulty in expressing it and, fundamentally, you would wish your biography to be written with effort, with pleasure, with hesitation, with a certain amount of touching-up, and also with a strict care for truth—a care not only for truths of fact (so far as the unfortunate biographer can attain them) but for that profounder truth which is poetic truth.

I believe that we are powerless to do more for great men than what we could wish to be done for ourselves. Truth? Yes, we must follow it with all our soul. *Σὺν ὅλῃ τῇ ψυχῇ εἰς τὴν ἀληθείαν ἰτέον* should be the motto of every historian. With all our soul—that is, with all our attention, with all our respect, with all our intelligence, but also with such faculties of artistic divination as we may possess. It would be dangerous and absurd to try to establish too close a parallelism between the exact sciences and the historical sciences. "Can we know the truth about a man?" we asked at the beginning. No, we can try to fix those changing lights and shades, we can try to produce the sound of that individual and authentic note, but it is a truth of a kind totally different from that which is pursued by the chemist or the physicist.

Such is our reply to the first question.

Now let us come to the second. To what degree is it possible to study an epoch of history in the course of writing a man's life? To what degree is it true to make a man the central figure of an epoch? Morley puts this point very well at the beginning of his *Life of Gladstone*:

Every reader will perceive that perhaps the sharpest of all the many difficulties of my task has been to draw the line between history and biography—between the fortunes of the community and the exploits, thoughts, and purposes of the individual who had so marked a share in them. In the case of men of letters, in whose lives our literature is admirably rich, this difficulty happily for their authors and for our delight does not arise. But where the subject is a man who was four times at the head of the government—no phantom, but dictator—and who held this office of first minister for a longer time than any other statesman in the reign of the Queen, how can we tell the story of his works and days without reference, and ample reference, to the course of events over whose unrolling he presided, and out of which he made history?

The biographer takes an individual man as a

central figure and makes the events of the period begin and end with him; they must all revolve round him. Biography is to history as the Ptolemaic system, which makes the stars revolve round the sun, is to the system of Galileo, which considers the planet only in its relation to the universe. Does this arbitrary attitude condemn biography as a historical work? No, for since history cannot, like physical science, examine what happens in a closed system, all histories are themselves subject to arbitrary limitations. If a history of France is written, the history of the world will again be made to revolve round France, just as the author of a Life of Wellington makes England revolve round Wellington. If we trust to Plutarch, we shall see Greece and Rome directed by some thirty intelligent wills—a state of things palpably absurd and inconsistent with the normal life of nations. According to the historical determinism of a Karl Marx, for instance, the mere intention to write a biography is a crime against truth; but the Marxists have committed this crime by their own biographies of Karl Marx and of Lenin. Clearly, then, it is inevitable.

The change of form thus imposed on history will be greater in proportion to the greatness of the individual man. Let us take an example from antiquity[1]. The history of the time of Alexander is known to us almost entirely through the biographies of Plutarch and Arrian. Consequently this fragment of history has always been incompletely treated. Obsessed by the vision of Alexander, historians have neglected to study the evolution of Macedon—how it had borrowed from the civilisation of Greece the sources of its strength—industry, a navy, armaments; and not the sources of its happiness—individual liberty and aesthetic culture. Macedon was to the rest of Greece what America is to Europe to-day. This is the key to the explanation of the Macedonian empire, which broke up of itself as soon as moral decadence, following in the train of culture, set in. This obsession by the personality of Alexander has also prevented the historian from realising the condition of the Persian empire before its fall. This empire had no military strength, as may be seen from the Retreat of the Ten Thousand, and as it appears to have suffered little from internal dissension, we must conclude that it enjoyed peaceful

[1] I am indebted for some valuable suggestions on this subject to M. Jean Prévost. For a Marxist theory of history see also A. L. Rowse's remarkable little book, *On History*.

prosperity to a high degree—a fact which the Greek and Plutarchian view of Alexander's civilising conquest has deliberately neglected. Thus the biographer's error—an error due to the very nature of his task—will have been to conceal whole peoples under the shadow of a man, and to present a man as the necessary and sufficient reason for events which transcend him.

If biographies were the sole source of history, one would get the idea that history was made up of individual opponents whose struggles produced the events of the period. The opposition between Gladstone and Disraeli, a very attractive theme for a biographer, is important only if it is made clear that below it lay the corresponding strata of the English social structure. The amateur biographer would, indeed, end by building up a history lacking in chronological continuity and in unity of development; and, owing to the need of representative men, the result would be an Emersonian morality and a Caesarian theory of politics.

On the other hand, consider what a unity, and I would add what beauty, there may be in a fragment of history, which contains no biographies and in which biographers have been obliged to start from history and from nothing else—I mean a fragment such as the Peloponnesian War. There no personal record occurs to mar the objectivity of Thucydides, but the very simplicity of such a eulogy is proof of its falseness. The complete agreement of historians on the subject of the Peloponnesian War would be ruined if, for example, there was in existence a biography of Cleon written by a democratic historian.

As always, it is difficult to deduce a general rule. In certain instances it is true that the personal action of one man has changed the life of a country. Between 1800 and 1815 the life of France was closely bound up with that of Napoleon[1]. On the other hand, in the case of Queen Victoria, Mr Strachey has wisely made his book a personal portrait rather than a large historical picture. The influence of the queen on English politics was certainly considerable, but she was only one amongst many other factors.

It is interesting to watch our own times because there we can seize upon history in the making. In

[1] Professor Trevelyan has written an essay, *If Napoleon had won the battle of Waterloo.* The argument of Rowse and of the Marxist historians is that this victory would not have greatly changed the history of the world. On the other side, see Renouvier's *Uchronie*, a fine book, too little known.

two cases at any rate I have been brought to conclude that the personal action, the character of a man, may become the determining factor in the phenomena of general history. One is the creation of French Morocco by Lyautey. There we may see, perfectly clearly, a country modelled by a single man and becoming, in fact, an enlarged representation of a man's personality. The other is the financial relief of France by M. Poincaré in 1925. But in both cases the statesman and the empire-builder fill the centre of the picture only for quite a short time. To fix them there for the whole of their lives would be to make an artificial picture. The biographer must not try to play the historian too long. Their objectives are different. Biography is the story of the evolution of a human soul; history should be for him what it is for the portrait-painter, the background against which he sets his model.

Is it not curious how the metaphor of the portrait-painter crops up as soon as one begins to talk of the biographer? And does not this resemblance itself help us to answer the question we put at the beginning of this lecture? "Ought biography to be a science?" we asked. We might as well ask whether the portrait-painter ought to be a scholar.

The reply is obvious: the portrait-painter should be a man of integrity, he should aim at a likeness, he should know the technique of his craft, *but his objective is the painting of the individual, whereas science is concerned only with the general.* And our reply accords with that of Mr Strachey:

> That the question has ever been, not only asked, but seriously debated, whether History was an art, is certainly one of the curiosities of human inaptitude. What else can it possibly be? It is obvious that History is not a science; it is obvious that History is not an accumulation of facts, but the relation of them....Facts relating to the past, if they are collected without art, are compilations, and compilations, no doubt, may be useful, but they are no more History than butter, eggs, salt and herbs are an omelette.

CHAPTER FOUR

BIOGRAPHY AS A MEANS OF EXPRESSION

Chapter IV

BIOGRAPHY AS A MEANS OF EXPRESSION

IN our consideration of "biography as a work of art," I deliberately left on one side the most important aspect of the question. To-day we shall proceed to examine it. For the artist the work of art is, before everything else, a deliverance. The artist is a being who in the course of his life has accumulated emotions for which he has not been able to find any outlet in action. These emotions swell within him and fill his soul almost to bursting-point; it is when he feels the urgent need of freeing himself that the work gushes out from him with an almost spontaneous force. Art is for him a means of expression.

It is easy to see that the best books have been written under the domination of strong emotions of this kind. Of all the novels of Dickens, *David Copperfield* is certainly the most popular; it is the book by means of which Dickens was eventually able to unburden himself of the miseries of his childhood, of which the recollection troubled him the more because it filled him with shame and repulsion.

In a case like this, a work of art acts in something of the same way in which confession serves the psychoanalyst. What is true of Dickens is true also of Meredith, who expressed himself sometimes in the pages of *Harry Richmond* and sometimes of *Evan Harrington*. It is true also of George Eliot, who has let loose her childhood in *The Mill on the Floss*. Stendhal could not help revealing under a change of form, both in *La Chartreuse de Parme* and in *Le Rouge et le Noir*, those emotions of love and hatred, repressed since his childhood, but displayed for us, in a more direct form, in his diary or in *Henri Brulard*. Balzac himself tells his own story in *Le Lys dans la vallée*; Flaubert says: "Madame Bovary, 'tis myself!" and as for Marcel Proust, his novel is simply one long confession.

We may note in passing that this subjectivity of emotion in no way hinders the work of art from being objective. When we say that Dickens and Meredith have expressed their own feelings through the medium of their works, we do not in any way mean that in these works they have recorded their own histories. (We insisted the other day on the risk and the absurdity of strictly autobiographical interpretation.) What we do mean is that they chose a subject which gave them the opportunity of expressing emotions which they themselves had very keenly felt. Sometimes there is a wide gulf between the fictitious subject and the real subject. Little Nell gives Dickens the opportunity of displaying the profound grief into which he was plunged by the death of his young sister-in-law. But the two girls bore no resemblance to each other either in their way of life or in their surroundings. The one thing essential is that beneath an objective surface there should lie that vivid emotion which gives the book an intensity, a burning passion, which a work written in cold blood can never have.

Now let us enquire whether biography, like the novel and autobiography, can be a means of expression, whether it can be an opportunity for the expression of strong emotions which the author has felt, whether, like the art-forms of which we have just spoken, it can have the benefit of a passion within itself and, in short, whether this way of looking at it is legitimate and does not endanger truth. It is difficult to see why it should not be legitimate. We have remarked that, in the case of a novelist, it is often by quite indirect means and through the medium of characters very far removed by circumstances from himself, that he attains to self-expression. Why should not the biographer be able to attain this same power of expression through the medium of characters in actual life? Why should he not feel himself as deeply moved by Byron's as by Evan Harrington's life?

As a matter of fact, Meredith was roused to strong emotion by characters in real life, as he has shown by his portrait of Mrs Norton in *Diana* and of Lassalle in *The Tragic Comedians*. Between such novels as these and biography properly so called the difference is small indeed.

May I now, by your leave, be guilty of a breach of your conventions and make, here and now, a public confession? I am well aware of the difficulties of such a course. I know that there is nothing more distasteful in any country in the world than to speak of oneself and of one's own works, that in particular there is nothing so un-English, and moreover that, even outside England, there is nothing more dangerous. If we confess ourselves satisfied with our own work, we are thought to be intolerably conceited; if we speak but humbly of them, every low-minded person will at once suspect us of mock humility. Nevertheless, in spite of all the danger, I feel myself compelled to take the risk; for, being in need of examples, it seems to me altogether more reasonable to attempt to show you the mechanism which has set in motion a man whom I may claim to know rather than a mechanism but little known to me which it would be more difficult for me to take to pieces.

I propose then to endeavour to show you very briefly how I was led to choose the life of Shelley and afterwards the life of Disraeli. At first sight it may seem strange that a Frenchman, with no particular training in English studies, should conceive the idea of writing a Life of Shelley. He could have no claim to bring fresh documents to light; he could not pretend to tell that beautiful story in a form better than the perfect form given to it by Dowden. Can he really have felt an overmastering need of writing the Life? And, if so, what were the secret springs which were at the bottom of this desire?

When I read a short Life of Shelley for the first time, I experienced a keen emotion. I will tell you why. I had just left the *lycée* and was full of philosophical and political ideas which, *mutatis mutandis*, represented just those ideas which possessed Shelley and his friend Hogg at the time of their arrival in London. Then, as circumstances rather brusquely forced me into action, I found my ideas in conflict with my experience. I had wanted to apply to my emotional life those rational systems which I had formed in the abstract in the course of my study of the great philosophers; but on all sides I had encountered material things, alive and sensitive, and they would not accommodate themselves to my logical system. I had been the cause of suffering and I had suffered myself. I was at once irritated by my past youthfulness and indulgent towards it, since I knew that it could not have been otherwise. I longed to expose it, to pillory it, and to explain it at the same time. Well, Shelley had experienced such checks as seemed to me to be somewhat of the same nature as my own; of course, his life had had a hundred times more of grace and greatness than mine, but I knew that in the same circumstances and at the same age I should have made the same mistakes. The pride and certainty of youth were succeeded in me by a lively need of pity and here too I discovered traces of Shelley as he was towards the end, after the loss of his children. Yes, in very truth I felt that to tell the story of his life would be in some measure a deliverance for myself. My first idea was to try to make a novel out of the life, to place the story of Shelley and Harriet and Mary in a modern setting. I actually wrote the novel; but it was not a good novel and my Shelley continued to torment me. Gradually I read everything that had been written about him, all his letters, all letters written by his friends, and at last I took the plunge. Was I right? I don't know. I don't think so. I don't like the book any longer. In my eyes it is spoilt by an ironic tone which came from the fact that the irony was aimed by myself at myself. I wanted to kill the romantic in me; and, in order to do it, I scoffed at it in Shelley, but I loved it while I scoffed. Good or bad, the book was written with pleasure, even with passion; and now I think you will begin to realise what I understand by biography considered as a means of expression.

The romanticism of Shelley was the romanticism of a very young man. But what happens to the romantic who does not die before the age of thirty in the bay of Spezzia? How does he come to reconcile the dreams of youth with the life of action which he is almost invariably forced to lead in his maturity? This was the problem that now troubled me and

I looked for a hero who might enable me to handle him in the same way. One day I read in Maurice Barrès that the most interesting life of the nineteenth century was that of Disraeli. I knew it a little, but not at all well. I read the *Life* by Froude, then Monypenny and Buckle's, then most of the memoirs of the period, and then Disraeli's own letters and novels. The more I read, the more I felt that I could find in Disraeli a hero in whom I should have a passionate interest. I had to deal with what was for me an entirely new character—the romantic who is at the same time a man of action; a man who succeeds in the temporal sense of the word but fails in the spiritual sense, and at his death remains a romantic—impenitent but not victorious.

I had no love for the young Disraeli with his gold chains, his elaborate waistcoats, his ambition. But I had immense sympathy for the Disraeli who discovered the opposition of a hostile world, for the Disraeli so grossly attacked by second-rate opponents, for the Disraeli who stuck to his guns and never accepted defeat, for the Disraeli who was the tender husband of Mary Ann and the faithful friend of John Manners, and above all for the old Disraeli, with his body enfeebled, but his heart still young.

I almost felt that it was through him that I learnt, without ever having felt it myself, the meaning of old age and of the approach of death—a piece of hard and inevitable schooling. At the same time I felt that through Disraeli I could express a political doctrine which was exactly what I was seeking—I mean a democratic conservatism, a combination of a great respect for tradition and for all that humanity has accomplished in the past, with a care for the happiness of the multitude and a desire for orderly reform. Being unable, for very many reasons, to lead a life of political activity myself, I took a passionate pleasure in joining in the struggle by donning the mask of a face that appealed to me. Here again you begin to realise, I think, what I understand by biography considered as a means of expression.

And may I add what I should like to do now? I would like to study, in a third manifestation, the reconciliation of an incurable romanticism of youth with the perfect serenity of a purified philosophy. What mask should one assume to allay this conflict? I can see two possible choices: Goethe and Meredith. Goethe begins his life with Werther, that is, in the full tide of romantic enthusiasm, and towards the end of it attains an equilibrium. In Meredith I find something profoundly interesting, namely, that he is a man who tried to re-fashion his character by his works and very nearly succeeded. Yes, I believe that a Life of Meredith written from this point of view might be a book profoundly interesting to write and remarkably instructive for the writer.

Once more I crave your pardon for having thus laid bare my own memories and projects. Biography is a means of expression when the author has chosen his subject in order to respond to a secret need in his own nature. It will be written with more natural emotion than other kinds of biography, because the feelings and adventures of the hero will be the medium of the biographer's own feelings; to a certain extent it will be autobiography disguised as biography. At any rate it would be so in that 'special case' in which the life of the hero should coincide with the life of the writer. You will see that this is scarcely possible. In the first place, the hero is always greater than the biographer; secondly, a biographer never discovers the whole of his own character in a historical character. It is merely one aspect of his character that he discovers, and often a very fleeting, a very limited aspect.

Yet it is not necessary to have experienced an

emotion for a long time in order to be aware of it. To describe a country or a social group it is not necessary to spend one's whole life in it; on the contrary, those who have merely passed through it often bring back fresher and more vivid impressions.

There is no need for Byron's biographer to be, like Byron, a Don Juan; there is no need for him to have made a conquest of a Lady Caroline Lamb, a Lady Oxford, a Guiccioli; there is no need for him to have deserted a wife or fled to a foreign country. Fortunately for him, he has no need to adopt a Byronic attitude. But it will be well, if only for a short period, that there should one day come upon him a flash of comprehension that such an attitude is human. William Morris' biographer will not have the generosity of William Morris, but he will try to understand William Morris by the aid of recollecting his own best moments.

But whether it be a matter of a whole character or of fleeting and limited aspects of a character, the problem remains the same. Is it legitimate to make use in this way of indirect observation? Is it legitimate to employ the recollection of our own passions in the interpretation and explanation of those of a historical character? Do we not run the risk, in thus employing ourselves as proxies for someone else, of spoiling the picture of the man whose life we want to write?

At this point I begin to hear fierce criticism. All those who regard history as a collection of facts can contemplate such an idea with nothing but horror. What would Mr Gradgrind say? We all know Thomas Gradgrind, biographer:

> A man of realities. A man of facts and calculations. A man who proceeds upon the principle that two and two are four, and nothing over, and who is not to be talked into allowing for anything over. Thomas Gradgrind, sir—peremptorily Thomas—Thomas Gradgrind—with a rule and a pair of scales, and the multiplication table always in his pocket, sir, ready to weigh and measure any parcel of human nature, and tell you exactly what it comes to. It is a mere question of figures, a case of simple arithmetic.

Perhaps I should not be very badly frightened by Mr Gradgrind if he were alone, but I see with sadness and dismay that, with all his charm and for all his difference from Mr Gradgrind, Mr Nicolson is in the same camp; he, too, would certainly condemn such a scheme. "Undue subjectivity,"

Mr Nicolson would say[1]. Yes, certainly "undue subjectivity." But, while I care very little for Mr Gradgrind's esteem, I would give much for Mr Nicolson's and would like to try to convince him.

As a matter of fact, I am really less afraid of him than I have said, since I know very well that he has himself, and in the best parts of his work, been most "unduly subjective." How could he have been otherwise? We desire to understand human beings with a comprehension entirely different from that of the movements of electrons or the habits of birds. Why? Because we know that for these more delicate enquiries we have at our disposal the instrument of a more perfect process, the process of confronting another's emotions with our own. Do you remember the admirable opening of M. Paul Valéry's *Introduction à la Méthode de Léonard de Vinci*? It is at once the finest criticism and the finest justification of all biography which has in it an element of subtilty: "We think," he writes, "that a man has thought; and we can discover in his works the very thought which comes to him from us; we can re-fashion that thought in the image of our own."

There is the whole truth in a nutshell; we can

[1] *The Development of English Biography*, p. 10.

"re-fashion a thought in the image of our own," and indeed we have hardly any other means of doing so. Valéry goes on to explain very clearly that as a result of this it is easy for us to reconstruct an ordinary man whose motives and ideas were very much like our own, whilst for a man who has excelled in some particular direction we have much more difficulty in imagining his spiritual progress. Next he explains that, having created a certain idea of a man of genius out of all the material available, he cast about for the name which should best suit it, and that no name seemed more appropriate to the man he had conceived than that of Leonardo da Vinci.

Thus, for Valéry, character is reduced to coincidence; but to him this pattern of an intellectual life is superior to a series of doubtful anecdotes, commentaries, letters, and dates. "Erudition of that kind," he says, "would simply falsify the wholly hypothetic purport of this essay. I am familiar with it, but for my purpose it is essential that I should not refer to it." That is an extreme case and would be ours if, for example, we said: "I want to write the history of a novelist who hammers out his own moral self by the help of his novels. It happens that the name of this novelist is George Meredith. But it is a pure coincidence and what really interests me is a theoretic novelist, not the man George Meredith." Only a Valéry has at once the courage and the right to put the problem of history in this abstract form, but every introspective biographer, whether he wishes it or not, is to some slight degree brought to a similar intellectual position.

A young French writer, who was asked by a publisher for a Life for a series of biographies, replied: "Certainly, but I don't know any history. You choose a character. All I demand is that it shall be a man or a woman who had a consistent desire to give a certain direction to his, or her, life and was always brought up against a closed door." There again we find, in its simplest form, the need for expression which will permeate the subject chosen with that deep-seated passion which alone perhaps has the potentiality of a work of art.

I realise very clearly, believe me, the dangers inherent in this type of biography. In his desire for self-expression and self-exposition, in his sympathy with, or antipathy to, a character (for his strong feeling may be one of antipathy, as in Mr Strachey), the biographer runs the risk of unwittingly defacing historical truth. To the extent to which he does so, his method is condemned and Mr Nicolson is justified—"undue subjectivity." Before everything else, history, or what we think we know of it, must be respected. To publish a biography, to announce it as a biography and not as a novel, is an announcement of authentic facts and the first thing that is due from a biographer to his reader is truth. He has no right to construct a hero according to his own needs and desires. He has no right to invent conversations and incidents. He has no right to omit certain facts because they do not fit in with his psychological structure; but it does seem possible in certain rare cases, if the choice is fortunate and well suited to the author's temperament, that the biographer may be able to express some of his own feelings without misrepresenting those of his hero.

But this identity of temperament is naturally rare and few heroes lend themselves to such treatment. It is hard to imagine a man who should write a Life of the Duke of Wellington by such a method, still less a Life of Henry VIII. But if this perfect congruence, this interchangeability of author and hero, is rare, I believe that it is almost impossible to write a biography without the biographer being compelled, in certain aspects and at certain times, to feel as his hero did. Otherwise how could he understand him? Long ago Livy laid down the rule: *Antiqua scribenti antiquus fit animus*. The soul of any man who writes a Life of Carlyle becomes, at any rate at certain moments, like Carlyle's. If he is incapable of such sympathy of feeling, he will write a detestable Carlyle.

In every psychological truth there is, and there must be, an element of divination. Critical reasoning alone will not make a man understand why Byron did not like Lady Caroline Lamb; by a long course of reading, by thorough familiarity with the letters, he must cultivate reactions similar to Byron's and then, all at once, his character will be illumined by a bright light from within because for one instant, however short, he has coincided with the man himself.

"Ah, but still your method is dangerous," the historians will say. We are well aware of it. It is *very* dangerous; it requires to be handled with infinite care, with absolute honesty, and with a fixed desire never to alter a single fact. There is only one argument in its favour, but that is all-powerful: *there is no other method*. We can understand a fact of science by analysis and synthesis; we cannot understand a human being by an exhaustive compilation of detail, because a human being represents an infinite complexity and, if we had centuries of life in front of us, we could never come to the end of this complexity. We get our understanding by a *coup d'état.*

And what of the reader? He, too, seeks in biography a means of expression:

"The very real pleasure which the intelligent reader to-day derives from biography," says Mr Nicolson, "proceeds in general from no very active energy of thought; his responses are stirred by languid processes of identification and comparison. He identifies himself with certain characters in a biography, and he compares his own feelings and experiences with theirs. This process, as Lord Oxford has remarked, is very pleasurable. It brings comfort, it enlarges sympathy, it expels selfishness, it quickens aspiration."

There too is mimicry, but mimicry in the opposite sense. The biographer makes himself like his hero in order to understand him; the reader, in order to copy his actions. There is no greater influence on men's conduct than the knowledge of the conduct of others. "Since that has been done, I can do it," says the reader to himself. As one reads the history of Napoleon, it is remarkable to observe how the study of Plutarch influenced both him, and, in general, all the men of the French Revolution. Then, three generations later, we realise the influence of the history of the Revolution itself upon the French politicians of the Left: one fancies himself a Danton; another a Saint-Just; another a Mirabeau. You may observe also what an influence the life of Caesar and of other great men of religious action—including even that of Loyola—exercised on the development of the young Disraeli.

Or suppose we contemplate ourselves. Most of us, I imagine, are not fired by ambition; in the souls of most of us great political careers do not touch a responsive chord. Yet, in spite of this, we do feel that the reading of Lives exercises some moral influence upon us. This is often a salutary influence, since the men of whom Lives are written are nearly always men above the common level and they lift us above the everyday cares of life into a region where creative action is freer and thought more lofty.

After reading the Life of Beethoven or of Ruskin

or of Goethe we do not of course feel ourselves to be on a level with them, but we all realise that in every human soul there is an element which understands and approves their noblest aspirations. We say to ourselves that in them too the stamp of greatness may at first have been in danger of obliteration in a wilderness of desires and conflicting passions. We feel that, if we cultivated this little patch of ground, and protected it against encroaching foliage, we too might succeed first in saving and then in extending it. Just as one rises from the reading of a great novel—*War and Peace* or *Middlemarch* or *Mrs Dalloway*—so one rises from the reading of a great Life a better man.

Consequently, whether we like it or not, biography is a type of literature which, more than any other, touches close upon morality. Of course, as we have just remarked, the novel also arouses powerful feelings; every work of art, in so far as it arouses the emotions and thereby the desire to act, touches upon morality. But biography comes much more closely to it, because the credibility of the narrative and the reader's conviction of the real existence of the people in the narrative make its influence immensely stronger. A child reading

Oliver Twist says to himself, "What a splendid little boy is Oliver Twist!" but does he really believe that a human being can maintain that perfection through a series of such adventures? A young Frenchman reading about the exploits of Jean Bart, or a young Englishman reading about those of Nelson, knows that the stories are true. The emotion aroused is perhaps less lively than that provoked by a novel, but the influence upon conduct is stronger.

Further, this influence is not always for the good. The psychology of imitation is such that a human being sometimes imitates another of whom he does not approve. Just as it behoves us to avoid linking ourselves to friends whose lives are reprehensible, since, as we say, "the example is contagious," so I believe we ought, in our reading, to avoid association with dangerous characters. Every man who undertakes a biography, though he may be the most a-moral of writers and though he may hold the very word 'morality' in horror, propounds, whether he wishes it or not, a rule of life based on individual examples. I am convinced that in the next few years we shall see in France the development of a phenomenon of which I already observe the first signs, namely, a renaissance of romantic sentiment. Many

Lives are being written in France at the present time. The public reads them eagerly. But there is a special vogue of the Lives of the great romantics, because such Lives abound in emotional drama. Undoubtedly the reading of such Lives is having a powerful influence on a generation which, at the end of the war, had, without knowing it, all the elements of romanticism within itself, just like the generation of 1815.

If the reader were moved to imitate in great men simply that which made them great, the influence would be all to the good; but unfortunately this does not always happen. Pascal, in his *Pensées*, gives the reason for this imitation of "the less good":

> The example of Alexander's chastity has not made as many chaste men as his drunkenness has made drunkards. There is no shame in being less virtuous than he was, and it seems excusable not to be more vicious. A man feels that he is not wholly sunk in the common vices of humanity when he sees himself sharing the vices of these great men; yet he loses sight of the fact that they themselves are thereby part of the common human stock. He touches them just at the point where they are in touch with the common people; for however exalted they may be, they still are linked with

common humanity at some point. They are not suspended in the air, far removed from our society—no, no. If they are greater than we are, it is because their heads are lifted higher; their feet reach down to ours. There they are all on the same level and the same earth supports them; and by this excess they are similarly brought as low as ourselves, as low as smaller men, as low as children, as low as beasts.

An important point to note is that even if the life recorded is that of a man of great character, and even if the reader of it is capable of understanding that character, a biography will always dispense an individualist, and never a social, morality. Those individual men who have made sufficient stir in political or literary history to become the subjects of biographies, have generally become so by being exclusively occupied with themselves or with their works. This is very striking in the biographies of great writers. Even in an apparently sociable man like Dickens one sees at once that his egoism was terrible. As soon as the book on which he was engaged showed signs of declining in pace and quality, he began to blame his family and the place where he was living—he must leave, not in a week, not in two days, but at once. Consider Tolstoy's life impartially, in the light of his children's records and of the short autobiography of the Countess Tolstoy, and there too you will see how there were no limits to the increasing dominance of a strong personality. The natural result is that the reader who feels that he has the slightest touch of genius in any particular direction, finds himself, after reading great men's Lives, impelled towards an urgent need of independence and to a contempt of the conventions of civilised society.

This applies all the more strongly, even in the case of men of quiet, modest, unambitious temperament—like Pasteur, for instance, or Darwin—since biography preserves especially those of their actions which differentiated them from other men and made their personalities stand out in a high relief which the ordinary man does not possess and which certainly was not visible to their own contemporaries.

If you read the official Lives of Herbert Spencer, you will not find in them that strange old man engrossed in painting over the flowers of his carpet with red ink, the old man as he was known to the two charming old maids with whom he spent several years towards the end of his life, the authoresses of *Home Life with Herbert Spencer*.

I am well aware that someone may reply, "It is a great deal better that it should be so. How does it concern us, if we are forming a judgment on a philosophy or even on a philosopher, to know that he attached great importance to the colour of his carpet or the thickness of his socks?"

Well, I'm not sure. It is always dangerous to give, as an example of a possible life, a life which has become unreal as a result of too much being left out. I fully believe that the truth about a man ought primarily to contain all that goes to make his greatness, but I also believe that we should not always neglect the elements of littleness, for it is in the conquest of such elements that greatness often consists.

We may now return to the moral effect of biography. It arouses in us the feeling of greatness; by its display of the power of the individual it gives us confidence; there may be a danger in its always having an exciting, rather than a soothing, effect. At the same time, if it can show us, side by side with the tragic events of a life, the calm and oblivion which follow them; if it can show us, side by side with great ambitions, the vanity of their realisation, it may also bring peace to our souls. There is at once great beauty and great tranquillity in the picture of Ruskin in his old age sitting by his window, looking vaguely at the clouds and murmuring "Beautiful... beautiful...." A biographer, such as Mr Strachey, who has the power to diffuse through his record of facts the poetic idea of Destiny, of the passage of Time, of the fragility of human fortune, brings us in fact a secret comfort.

For the full expression of this sublimated morality the biographer must never consciously think about morals. "In 1840," says Mr Nicolson, "moral earnestness again intervened, and the art of English biography, until 1881, declined." It is perfectly true. Every biographer should write on the first page of his manuscript: "Thou shalt not judge." Moral judgment may be hinted at; but as soon as it is formulated, the reader is recalled to the sphere of ethics and the sphere of aesthetics is lost to him.

Mr Strachey, in a remarkable article on Carlyle, shows that the ambition to be a prophet was extremely detrimental to Carlyle's value as a historian:

> To be a prophet is to be a moralist and it was the moral preoccupation in Carlyle that was particularly injurious to his artistic instincts....Morality,

curiously enough, seems to belong to that class of things which are of the highest value, which perform a necessary function, which are in fact an essential part of the human mechanism, but which should only be referred to with the greatest circumspection. Carlyle had no notion that this was the case and the result was disastrous. In his history, especially, it is impossible to escape from the devastating effects of his reckless moral sense.

Perhaps it is the platitude of such a state of mind, that is its most exasperating quality. Surely one thinks poor Louis XV might be allowed to die without a sermon from Chelsea. But no! The opportunity must not be missed; the preacher draws a long breath and expatiates with elaborate emphasis upon all that is most obvious, about mortality, crowns and the futility of self-indulgence.

... There is an imaginative greatness in his conception of Cromwell, for instance, but all is spoilt by an overmastering desire to turn the strange Protector into a moral hero after Carlyle's own heart, so that after all the lives are blurred, the composition is confused, and the picture unconvincing.

Yes, all moral pre-occupation in a work of art, whether it be a novel or a biography, kills the work of art. As soon as we attempt to prove something, we prove nothing. But that is not to say that great moral themes may not be of the very stuff of the work. Think once more of the lyrical dramas of Wagner; we cannot say that the Tetralogy proves anything, but great themes run all through it: the tyranny of gold, redemption by love—themes which are still further developed by that language, at once confused and clear, which we call music. I believe that the same might apply to a great biography, inspired and sustained by powerful passions. It must not have a moral aim, but it is good that we should from time to time hear within it the trumpet-call of Destiny.

CHAPTER FIVE

AUTOBIOGRAPHY

Chapter V

AUTOBIOGRAPHY

AT the beginning of a course of lectures on a single subject, the lecturer looks for some central idea which he may use as a guiding thread throughout the course. When he has thoroughly turned the subject over and has begun by considering it from three very different aspects, he eventually perceives what will give him his unity. The whole course is like one of those great parks with a castle in the middle. The park is well planned; all the paths lead, as it were, to the centre of a star. When we enter by a small gate, we do not know at first which direction to take; we try the first, the second, and the third path; and then we realise that they all point to the existence of some invisible centre and the plan of the whole estate becomes clear to us. This, I think, is what is happening to us. We have approached Biography by the paths of "work of art," of "means of expression," of "science," and we realise that they all lead us to one central question: Is it possible to know the truth about a man? Up to now the answer appears to be negative. But there remains one form which might give us grounds for hope—I mean the form of autobiography.

"Every man's life," said Dr Johnson, "should be best written by himself." Was the great doctor right? It would seem, on the face of it, of course, that every man knows the facts of his own life fairly accurately and that all he has to do is to be quite candid in giving a complete record of them. In particular, it would seem that if he wants to write a psychological biography he should be better able than anyone else to recall the inner stirrings, the motives of his actions and, still more, the secrets of those actions which he would have liked to accomplish, had not circumstances prevented him. So it seems at first sight. But on further reflection we see that we must make important reservations. There are several causes which tend to make autobiographical narrative inaccurate or false:

(1) The first is the fact that we forget. As soon as we attempt to write our own life-history, most of us discover that we have forgotten a great part of it. For many of us, childhood is a complete blank. For my own part, up to the age of seven or eight, I can recall only a few outstanding memories. They appear as tiny isolated pictures surrounded

on both sides by the dark strands of forgetfulness. Perhaps this is a peculiar personal weakness of mine, for certain authors seem to be able to remember further back. Tolstoy retained a vivid impression of what he felt when, at the age of six months, he was put into a wooden tub to be washed; he remembered the smell of the soapy wood and the slippery, greasy feeling beneath his feet. Sir Edmund Gosse, in his *Father and Son*, has clear and obviously authentic memories of his childhood. Goethe remembers quite well his walks as a child along the walls of Frankfort; it is curious to observe how even as a child he had a longing to plunge into a thousand different ways of life, and how, as he contemplated at this period the little gardens of the Frankfort bourgeoisie, he received impressions which were already those of the man of letters.

Anthony Trollope gives an admirable description of his impressions as a schoolboy of seven years old:

I remember well, when I was still the junior boy in the school, Dr Butler, the head-master, stopping me in the street, and asking me, with all the clouds of Jove upon his brow and all the thunder in his voice, whether it was possible that Harrow School was disgraced by so disreputably dirty a little boy as I! Oh, what I felt at that moment! But I could not look my feelings. I do not doubt that I was dirty;—but I think that he was cruel.

Trollope remembers this feeling because it was a vivid one and in this way childhood often seems to a grown man to be nothing but a succession of rare incidents, namely, those which produced such a violent impression that the nervous shock of it still has the power to make us tremble after the lapse of years.

Thus a childhood passed in a period of war or revolution leaves more abundant memories than a calm and happy childhood.

In Benjamin Haydon's *Autobiography* we see how strong an impression was made upon him by the French Revolution and how, round about 1794, little English boys used to amuse themselves with miniature guillotines for cutting off the head of Louis XVI twenty times a day.

Sometimes memories are one degree removed. Our parents or our grandparents tell us the story of our childhood and our own recollections are in fact recollections of their narratives. Herbert Spencer, who, in the course of writing his autobiography, endeavoured to contemplate himself from the point of view of the scholar, puts it very well:

Of incidents in childhood, my remembrances have assumed that secondary form which I suspect they mostly do in advanced life—I simply remember that I once remembered—There was a little sister Louisa, a year my junior, who died at two years old; and playing with her in the garden left faint pictures which long survived. There also survived for many years, recollections of getting lost in the town, into which I had wandered to find the house of some friends to whom I was attached; the result being that the Crier was sent round to find me. My most vivid childish recollection, however, worth mentioning because of its psychological interest, is that of being left alone for the first time. Everyone was out save the nurse, who had been left in charge of me; and she presently seized the occasion to go out too, locking up the house and leaving me by myself. On one evening every week, which happened to be the evening in question, it was the custom to ring a peal on the bells of the chief church in Derby, All Saints'; and while I was suffering the agonies of this first experience of solitude, its bells were merrily going. The effect was to establish in me so strong an association, that all through the earlier part of my life, and even in adult years, I never heard these bells without a feeling of sadness coming over me.

Yes, all that remains to us of our childhood consists of just such tiny things—confused feelings mixed up with associations of which the origin is lost in obscurity. This is not enough to explain the complex individuality which we all acquire by the age of six or seven. Of the vast accession of vocabulary, ideas, and emotions; of our introduction to the world outside, of the successive pictures of society which are formed in the mental vision of a child—of all this we retain practically nothing; and so an autobiography of childhood is nearly always commonplace and untrue, even when the author himself is sincere.

This, moreover, is a reason for giving particular attention to the memoirs of anyone who has had the opportunity of preserving a faithful picture of this period of life. Mr Maurice Baring has described his own in a charming way in his *Puppet Show of Memory*, and I am extremely fond of the first pages of that fine autobiography, *Apostate*, by Forrest Reid.

The mechanism of forgetting operates all through life. We do not forget other periods so completely as we forget childhood, because the grown-up is established in a social frame and, as a result, his recollections are linked on to certain fixed realities which surround and absorb him. Nevertheless, if he can cut himself off completely from race and country, he may be genuinely oblivious of certain whole periods of his life. Even when he remembers, his recollection is incomplete. Suppose, for instance, that I try to call to memory the mobilisation of August, 1914. I discover certain pictures, certainly, but what do they represent? A few minutes, perhaps. All the rest, all the long hours of suspense and agony have vanished for ever. We realise our capacity for forgetting when we come upon a fairly detailed note made upon some event which we actually witnessed. Then, when we read our own memoirs, the pictures do actually rise up before us. But we realise that, if we had not preserved the written testimony, we should have compiled a record that would have been not only incomplete, but inaccurate.

Hence a special value belongs to those memoirs which are jotted down in diaries—as in Haydon's *Autobiography*, for instance, which I mentioned just now. A diary pure and simple may seem wearisome owing to the monotony of its form, but fragments of diaries woven into the stuff of a narrative give it a remarkable feeling of authenticity. Furthermore, it is probable that many famous memoirs have been written with the help of diaries of an earlier date. It is impossible to imagine, for example, how Cardinal de Retz could, after fifteen or twenty years, have written his memoirs, in which he reproduced whole conversations with the queen or with Mazarin, if he had not made use on the one side of his own diary, and on the other of the parliamentary records.

In particular, we forget our dreams. We often forget them a few minutes after we wake. From a genuine autobiography they are wholly absent, and yet our lives and our thoughts are partly made up of the stuff of dreams. In fact, both dreams and reality are lacking in our narrative; for our days and nights consist of an infinity of images and sensations and the infinite is *ex hypothesi* inexhaustible. James Joyce writes the eight hundred closely packed pages of his *Ulysses* in order to record a single day in the life of a man, and he is still far from making it complete. What are we to say of the autobiographer who compresses twenty thousand days of his life into one or two volumes?

(2) The second factor which makes for deforma-

tion is deliberate forgetfulness on aesthetic grounds. If an autobiographer is also a gifted writer, he is tempted, whether he wishes it or no, to make the story of his life a work of art. To do this successfully, he finds that his material, even when winnowed by inspired forgetfulness, is still too vast. Take a diary like that of Pepys. It is highly amusing and we are devoted to it for a thousand reasons which are not literary reasons. To make it a work of art, we should have to blot out much of it. This is true also of Amiel. It is only a short diary which can retain both the charm of day-by-day candour and the artistic charm imparted to a narrative by the oneness of the writer's personality. This applies, for instance, to the admirable diary of Byron which has recently been re-edited by the good offices of Lord Ernle. But the Ravenna diary is the story of a few days. Byron's contemptuous laziness would not let him write thus for the whole of his life. The memoirs destroyed by Moore were probably memoirs only in form, resting on a foundation of convenient and necessary oblivion.

It has been well said by Herbert Spencer that throughout our lives memory discards, builds up, leaves out, and transforms the truth, since it leaves no place for everyday life, for simple events, for those calm periods in which nothing unexpected happens, periods which nevertheless form the essential stuff of human existence:

A biographer, or autobiographer, is obliged to omit from his narrative the common-place of daily life and to limit himself almost exclusively to salient events, actions and traits. The writing and the reading of the bulky volumes, otherwise required, would be alike impossible. But by leaving out the humdrum part of the life, forming that immensely larger part which it had in common with other lives, and by setting forth only the striking things, he produces the impression that it differed from other lives more than it really did. This defect is inevitable.

That is an acute and profound observation, and confirms what we said about the too strongly individualistic morality which is the outcome of all biography.

When we read the life of a man, we get the impression that his life was much more interesting, much more out of the common, than our own. Well, this is to a certain extent true, because the life is that of some great man; but only to a certain extent, since the wonderful events of which we read occupied only a few hours, perhaps, of the hero's life, whilst the rest of it was very much like our own. Memory is a great artist. For every man and for every woman it makes the recollection of his, or her, life a work of art and an unfaithful record.

(3) Forgetfulness is not the only means by which autobiography changes the face of truth. Another means is that perfectly natural censorship which the mind exercises upon whatever is disagreeable. Let us return for a moment to a narrative of childhood. If it has been discontented or shameful, it is virtually impossible for it to be sincerely related. We remember things when we want to remember them; we consign to oblivion anything that has hurt us—we change it, consciously at first; we make our narrative a little more pleasant, a little more lively, a little more exciting than the actual event. Our success in this encourages us to go further. Gradually we get to the stage of remembering only the narrative and forgetting the actual event, and in course of time the work of our imagination takes the place of those fainter pictures of a vanished reality. As an example of a childhood unconsciously transformed by a curious sense of shame, we may cite that of Disraeli, who, in all the autobiographical

fragments which he has left, maintains that his family came from Venice, whereas it belonged in fact to a little town called Forli. But Venice attracted Disraeli by virtue of its famous name, of its history, of its beautiful palaces, of the gold and the doves in the square of St Mark—and the process of substitution went on in his mind, doubtless in spite of himself.

"Swinburne," says Mr Harold Nicolson, "did not fail, on occasion, to adorn his family tree with certain decorative, but purely fictitious ancestors." He talked about the French elements in his blood, explained that these elements were derived from a Polignac, and even, when he particularly warmed to his subject, from the Marquis de Sade. It was not true—any more than it was true that the Cardinal de Retz belonged to an "old and illustrious" family, as he declared in his memoirs. There is a touching *naïveté* about such falsehoods; but they are falsehoods none the less and they change the face of truth.

(4) Another form of censorship is that which is operated by a sense of shame. Very few men have had the courage to tell the truth about their sexual life. Obviously one can point to Rousseau, who, in two or three passages, has been exceedingly frank.

But one may legitimately ask whether, in Rousseau's case, it is not a sort of exhibitionism which forces him to exaggerate his recollections of such matters. In any case, his example proves that such confidences strike us in a tender place. We think, as we read them, of that terrible idea of Swift's—a parliament of naked men; whether we like it or not, man with clothes on, civilised man, has become for us a truer picture than naked man. We are grateful to Benjamin Constant, who tells the story of his amours in his *Cahier Rouge*, for telling it decently. It is better in such matters to suggest than to describe. It is passion which has the quality of individuality—mere physiology is *banale*.

Further, how can the autobiographer tell the real truth about such things? Since he has chosen to write, he is an artist, he is a man who feels, like every artist, the need of escape; and if his narrative is to be a real escape, there must be for the author the pretext of a life more in keeping with his desires than his own life has actually been. To endow himself with this life, he will do what the novelist does; he will create it. The only difference between him and the novelist is that, as he creates it, he will say, and perhaps even believe, that it is his own, whilst the novelist is conscious of his creative act.

"The primary impulse of the artist," says Forrest Reid, "springs, I fancy, from his discontent and his art is a kind of crying for Elysium....I may promise to present it [the real world] and the people who lived in it without a rag of disguise, but I know I cannot keep my promise."

(5) Memory not only fails, whether by the simple process of time or by deliberate censorship; but, above all, it rationalises; it creates, after the event, the feelings or the ideas which might have been the cause of the event, but which in fact are invented by us after it has occurred. Actually, the event was the work of chance. In many instances we discover lofty, heroic motives for actions which we have performed unwittingly and unconsciously. Is it true that Caesar deliberately wished to cross the Rubicon? It is certain that Napoleon did not desire the 18th Brumaire. Read the memoirs of generals and compare the magnificently clear piece of construction which a battle becomes in the memoirs of the man who directed it with what the battle actually was. We have all seen a few battles. Before the beginning of the action, there was a clear plan, a

succession of advances, all carefully laid out by the staff-officers. But once the battle had begun, men came and went and ran about; telephone wires were cut; troops were scattered and a candid account would be a description of an appalling intellectual anguish. But the general will write in his memoirs: "I then debouched from the forest and decided to attack the enemy's left."

It is the same in political life. The tone of a questioner's voice, the quality of a conversation, are not without their influence on a decision; very often such feelings as those of love or friendship change the whole of a man's career; he changes his political party because he has married a wife who does not share his earlier ideas; he is converted himself and brings his philosophy up to date. Like Auguste Comte, he makes Woman the centre of his system because Clotilde de Vaux has entered into his life; if he is an economist, he juggles with figures and makes statistics declare what he knows will be pleasing to those who have become dear to him.

When the crisis is past, he looks back, rationalises, and says to himself: "I am a socialist, I am a positivist, I am a conservative....The development of my ideas was as follows. Such and such a process of reasoning convinced me." Later, in his old age, he finds himself (if he examines the past) in the presence of this series of incoherent and contradictory crises, and, since he cannot tolerate the idea of not being able to understand himself, he makes a system out of his life and organises it in order to make this system coherent.

Let us look at the case of Rousseau. It is important because the *Confessions* have been one of the sources from which other men have been inspired with the desire and with the courage to write their autobiographies. "I am setting out upon an enterprise which has no precedent and will have no imitators." In Rousseau's case we have both a confession which the writer wishes to be sincere to the point of humiliation, and also a series of letters written on a higher level of self-respect. Well, if we contrast the letters with the *Confessions*, we find that, so far as the first years of his life were concerned, Rousseau exaggerated his stupidity and mental slowness; his letters are much too intelligent to have been written by the little bumpkin whom he describes in the *Confessions*. Why? Perhaps he wanted to put his mind on a level with his own humble condition. Furthermore, Rousseau, at the age of fifty, is an independent republican and is longing to find in himself as a young man the first signs of this independence. As a matter of fact, up to the age of twenty-five he was just a pliable youth, very awkward and rather simple, with no strict principles at all.

In the *Confessions* he entirely omits to inform us—though it is perfectly clear in his letters—that it was a denial of justice on the part of the ambassador to whom he was secretary which first turned him to thoughts of nature and liberty. If he had had an intelligent chief, we should certainly not have had Rousseau—but Rousseau cannot admit it. The *Confessions* are "less a disinterested biography than a justificatory memoir[1]."

(6) There is one last cause of lack of sincerity in autobiographies, namely, the perfectly legitimate desire to protect those who have been our companions in the actions which we describe. Even if we have resolved to tell the whole truth about our own lives, we have no right to resolve to tell the whole truth about other people's—or at least we do not believe that we have any such right.

[1] Jean Prévost.

We should admit that Lord Byron had written a confession. We should have had the greatest difficulty in admitting that Byron had written, in a direct and non-fiction form, the confession of Caroline Lamb.

It is impossible, then, to retrieve the past; it is impossible not to change it unconsciously, and, further, it is impossible not to change it consciously. Such are the obstacles which make one fear that an authentic autobiography can never be written. The supreme autobiographer would need to possess the analytical genius and the perceptiveness of a Proust, a sense of the oneness of humanity, such as that of Fernandez, and, beyond all this, an impartiality and an objective attitude in relation to his own life which would enable him to review it in the same detached way as Bergotte (Proust's hero) reviewed the lives of his commonplace characters.

Is it impossible to conceive of such a person? No, but we must remember that up to now he has not appeared—which is a pity.

"Oh," said Jane Carlyle, "if I might write my own biography from beginning to end, without reservation or false colouring—it would be an invaluable document for my countrywomen in more than one particular. But 'decency forbids'!"

Still, there are some examples of entirely satisfactory autobiography. You have one in England, one published in the life-time of its author. I mean *Father and Son*, by Edmund Gosse. In that book the motive which impelled Sir Edmund Gosse to write appears to have been the usual motive of the novelist—the desire for freedom, for deliverance. But the tone of it is so fair, the portraits so faithful, the detachment so magnificent, that the reader cannot at any single moment feel shocked. *Father and Son* contains a proof, and a very rare proof, that an unfettered examination of one's self is possible.

Let me suggest without delay the reasons that made this success possible. *Father and Son* is an intellectual biography, the history of how a man's ideas and intelligence were developed. The same applies to a book which has the same charm and sometimes the same tone as *Father and Son*—I mean *The Autobiography of Mark Rutherford.* Rarely has a man spoken with more naturalness of his religious life, of the genesis of his doubts, of his ideas about love and death. It is true that in this case the story of Mark Rutherford had slightly disguised the autobiography and that it differed from the story of William Hale White, its creator. But it differs only in matters of fact; the spiritual confession is authentic. Here again the success is complete.

If we now proceed to posthumous autobiographies we note at once that the only perfect examples are those in which the author has described only the development of a mind. You have John Stuart Mill, you have Newman, you have Gibbon, you have—a little below perfection—Herbert Spencer; we have the *Souvenirs d'Enfance et de Jeunesse* of Ernest Renan. Why are these intellectual autobiographies superior to the rest? First, I think, because everything which concerns the life of the spirit is apparently less, but actually much more, conscious than anything else in our lives; secondly, because we have less intellectual reticence than sentimental or sensual reticence. We may regard certain of our actions or of our feelings with a sense of shame; we rarely feel ashamed of our ideas. When we take up our pen to write, we undertake to explain them because we regard the steps by which we have reached an intellectual position as perfectly legitimate. If we did not believe them to be legitimate, we should think otherwise. Hence, for example, comes the quiet nobility of a book like John Stuart Mill's *Autobiography*. Nothing happens. It appears as though a whole life may be spent in the pursuit of accurate thinking. The author's detachment is complete. When he encounters a man different from himself, he judges him with admirable serenity. I have no wish to burden you with quotations which you know better than I; I should like simply to read to you the few lines on Carlyle. Mill did not like him and was not made so as to understand him. Nevertheless, this is what he said of him:

I did not deem myself a competent judge of Carlyle. I felt that he was a poet, and that I was not; that he was a man of intuition, which I was not; and that as such, he not only saw many things long before me, which I could only when they were pointed out to me, hobble after and prove, but that it was highly probable he could see many things which were not visible to me even after they were pointed out. I knew that I could not see round him and could never be certain that I saw over him; and I never presumed to judge him with any definiteness, until he was interpreted to me by one greatly the superior of us both—who was more a poet than he, and more a thinker than I—whose own mind and nature included his and infinitely more.

The only objection one could make to a book like John Stuart Mill's would be this: Is it not artificial to isolate a man's intellectual development in this way? The reply is that it is not artificial in dealing with certain men for whom the intellectual life is everything. Spencer's case is slightly different. Spencer wanted not only to write an intellectual autobiography like John Stuart Mill, but at the same time to provide a scientific document dealing with a character whom he considered the most interesting of his age—to wit, himself.

It has seemed to me that a natural history of myself would be a useful accompaniment to the books which it has been the chief occupation of my life to write. In the following chapters I have attempted to give such a natural history. That I have fully succeeded is not to be supposed; but perhaps I have succeeded partially. At any rate, one significant truth has been made clear—that in the genesis of a system of thought the emotional nature is a large factor; perhaps as large a factor as the intellectual nature.

These few lines are very remarkable. The expression "natural history of myself" is worth remembering and would indeed constitute the autobiographer's ideal, if one could actually produce a "natural history of oneself."

But, nevertheless, you see how far, even in Spencer's case, this natural history is from being impartial. Spencer is full of the most praiseworthy scruples; he asks himself at great length whether one may, in an autobiography, speak well of oneself; for on the one hand, he says, if the writer omits to mention the incidents that have marked the progress of his character and his success, this omission diminishes the value of the narrative.

On the other hand, as they reflect some kind of honour on him, the mention of them appears indicative of vanity; though it may result from a desire to give a complete presentation, or from the feeling that against the debit items of the account it is but fair that the credit items should be placed. What, then, is to be done? At first sight it seems possible for one who narrates his own life and draws his own portrait to be quite truthful; but it proves to be impossible.

There are various media which distort the things seen through them, and an autobiography is a medium which produces some irremediable distortions.

And, in spite of all this conscientiousness, we cannot help thinking that Spencer has spoken a little too well of himself. The feeling of oppression by the personality of others is so strong in each of us, as soon as a tendency towards arrogance or conceit appears, that it is almost impossible to hear a man speaking about himself without feeling how intensely ludicrous he is. It is unjust, it may even be absurd, but it is so. There is nothing really very funny in the passage I am going to read to you, and yet we cannot hear it without smiling:

Probably many readers of the foregoing pages will have been struck by the heterogeneity in my mental occupations and objects of interest....The products of mental action are then seen to range from a doctrine of State-functions to a levelling-staff; from the genesis of religious ideas to a watch escapement; from the circulation in plants to an invalid bed; from the law of organic symmetry to planing machinery; from principles of ethics to a velocimeter; from a metaphysical doctrine to a binding-pin; from a classification of the sciences to an improved fishing-rod joint; from the general Law of Evolution to a better mode of dressing artificial flies.

It is ludicrous to hear a man solemnly and

anxiously asking himself where his admirable faculty of exposition comes from:

I have an unusual faculty of exposition—setting forth my data and reasonings and conclusions with a clearness and coherence not common. Whence this faculty? My grandfather passed all his life in teaching, and my father, too, passed all his life in teaching.... No one will deny that I am much given to criticism. Along with the exposition of my own views there has always gone a pointing out of defects in the views of others. And, if this is a trait in my writing, still more is it a trait in my conversation. The tendency to fault-finding is dominant —disagreeably dominant. The indication of errors in thought and in speech made by those around, has all through life been an incurable habit,—a habit for which I have often reproached myself, but to no purpose. Whence this habit? There is the same origin as before. While one half of a teacher's time is spent in exposition, the other half is spent in criticism—in detecting mistakes made by those who are saying lessons, or in correcting exercises, or in checking calculations; and the implied powers, moral and intellectual, are used with a sense of duty performed. And here let me add that in me, too, a sense of duty prompts criticism; for when, occasionally, I succeed in restraining myself from making a comment on something wrongly said or executed,

I have a feeling of discomfort, as though I had left undone something which should have been done: the inherited tendency is on its way to become an instinct acting automatically.

Note that here Spencer tries to be severe upon himself. But Proust has remarked, and rightly remarked, that when we believe we are being particularly hard upon ourselves, we are still much less so than are other people towards us. Certain phrases we have used, which seem to us perfectly natural, are picked out and commented on as indications of selfishness or folly. Our actions are interpreted in a complex and frequently unjust fashion. Fortunately, we do not know it; for, if we did, we should never dare to say or do another thing. But when we attempt to draw our own portrait for other people, we must not be surprised if the portrait is not accepted as a likeness.

Spencer wanted to write a Natural History; other autobiographers have wanted to produce a work of literature. Sometimes, as with De Quincey, for example, this care for literary form has spoilt the simplicity of the work. In Gibbon's case we readily accept the noble style and the beautifully balanced phrases even at moments of emotion, since we feel that this sense of balance is part of Gibbon's personality. In his worst moments the phrase was for him an integral part of his life; it aroused feelings and passions, it soothed them with the gentle rocking of its majestically regular waves, and certainly it set them at rest. The reader of Gibbon cannot help feeling a sympathy for a writer who had found in his work the sovereign good. Gibbon's autobiography has a simple greatness which makes it one of the most charming books in the English language. But still it is not what we are looking for—a perfect representation of the man. It is a picture of an exceptional being, of a craftsman exclusively engaged in his craft. Who then will give us the whole man? Certainly no one amongst the autobiographers. Goethe was wise enough to give his autobiography the title, *Poetry and Truth*; and it is in fact almost impossible that a record of a life should not be a mixture of poetry and truth. It is so precious to us, this life of ours....How could those paltry happenings, so simple, so ordinary, seem anything but important to us, more important than anything else in the world, since they inspired in us such vivid emotions? We know that we shall have nothing else in the world except these forty, these sixty years; we should like them to be years of beauty or at least to have contained a few rare moments of perfection. When actual life does not give such moments, we create them, we reconstruct them—that is to say, we are, in the fullest sense of the word, poets.

Portrait-painters know well that a sitter is never satisfied with his own portrait, whilst the other portraits which he sees in the same studio strike him as excellent. Is this reprehensible vanity? No, it is because we have encountered the one face—our own—a thousand times in mirrors, in other people's expressions, in our own imagination. We know that it is imperfect; we know that it is ugly; but we are always hoping that by some temporary miracle the painter will faithfully translate that clumsy, futile goodwill which lies in each one of us. It is the same in portraits of moral character. The severest autobiography remains a piece of special pleading. "That I, or any man," said Trollope, "should tell everything of himself, I hold to be impossible. Who could endure to own the doing of a mean thing? Who is there that has done none?" Nor must we set up the cynics against Trollope in this regard—Cardinal de Retz, for instance, saying to the scandalised monks as he dictated his memoirs to them: "Go on, go on; I did it, and so there's no shame in telling it." For Retz himself is still a pleader, and so is Rousseau and so is Gide.

Once more we have set out upon a chase and once more the creature of the chase, Truth, has eluded us. In our final lecture we shall see whether it has not taken refuge in the novel.

CHAPTER SIX

BIOGRAPHY AND THE NOVEL

Chapter VI

BIOGRAPHY AND THE NOVEL

FOR the space of five hours we have together been in pursuit of a shadow which has been flying before us—the shadow which is the truth about a man. We asked ourselves whether the biographer could catch it; it appears that he cannot. Every time we thought to lay a hand upon the ghostly shoulder of the phantom, it split into two others which fled by different paths in opposite directions. On one side there ran the acts and the outward life of the man duly embodied in documents and evidence; one knew that he had travelled, that he had met such and such a woman, that he had delivered such and such a speech. On the other side there was his inner life, and it was this particularly which vanished just as we thought we had a hold upon it. Sometimes it seemed to materialise in the form of diaries, or letters, but then these documents roused suspicion. We felt that beneath them, very far beneath them, there was something else which we ought to have known, something else with which we were quite familiar in ourselves—the continuous flow of thoughts, the secret images passing through the mind, the chain of resolutions and regrets. But, alas, how can we know them? When we have to do with the dead whose bones lie in some wooden box, or whose ashes rest in an urn, thoughts and images are gone for ever and the most patient research will yield us nothing but dust.

Furthermore, when it happens that a diary and a contemporary account show us the intentions and the actual performance of our hero side by side, we find that they are contradictory. Just at the moment when we should have severely condemned him for his action, the candour of his intention disarms us. We are driven to declare that where our knowledge is confined to the action, it is almost impossible to interpret it. You know the story of Rossetti, who, when full of lively remorse for his selfish conduct towards his wife, decided, as a penance, to bury in his wife's tomb the poems which he had written since his marriage, poems which were to him the symbol of his guilt; and you know too that some months later, when he could not endure not being able to remember these poems and passionately desired to recover them, Rossetti could not resist the temptation of having the tomb re-opened and of taking his manuscript back. It is a terrible episode.

A novelist could make a moving story of it by showing us what went on in the soul of Rossetti during the time of his temptation and also during the execution of his plan[1]. But what can the biographer do? He knows so little....What was Rossetti thinking exactly? What were his feelings at the moment when he had made his first gesture—that of burying the manuscript? What were his feelings at the moment when he took his terrible decision? We do not know; we shall never know.

It is a disturbing thought for a biographer to contemplate what would have been his interpretation if a particular document, which might well have disappeared, had in fact disappeared. Shelley deserts his wife, Harriet, and goes off with Mary Godwin; there is the fact. It happens that we know, from different testimonies, that at that moment he suspected Harriet of unfaithfulness; it is the explanation of, and the excuse for, his conduct. But, if we had not these testimonies, as is perfectly conceivable, how cruel and inconsequent Shelley's conduct would seem!

Human beings only live in biography to the extent that others have seen and taken note of their

[1] M. Edmond Jaloux has in fact written this story.

actions. *Esse est percipi*, the old idealist philosophy used to say. Similarly, the hero of a biography exists only by means of the various little sketches made of him either by eye-witnesses or by himself, and it seems as though there is no real being beneath all these appearances. Nevertheless the real being does exist, too; we are convinced of it, because we know that we ourselves exist. But where can we find this real being? What hunter has ever been able to pursue two shadows at the same time? The biographer? Apparently not. But perhaps the novelist can[1]. The novelist can in fact place himself in a position which enables him to see two points of view at once. Think, for example, of the case of a soldier who, in the course of an attack, lies hidden in a shell-hole while he might be advancing and only rejoins his comrades a little later when the artillery barrage has been lifted. If he is found out by an officer, he will be reckoned as a coward, and, if his conduct becomes known to his biographer at a later date, the soldier will go down to history as wanting in courage. If the shirker is not found out, this particular action disappears entirely, so far as his biographer is concerned. But, from the point of view

[1] See Ramón Fernandez, *Messages*.

of the soldier himself, it is possible that at bottom he was full of courageous resolves. He is not a coward; he wanted to advance, but his body refused and somehow compelled him to remain where he was. Now the novelist may realise this; he may also be familiar with the officer's opinion, and he can express them both. So the complete evidence for a life can only be said to exist when we have both the evidence of the spectator and the evidence of the actor together, and when, as Ramon Fernandez says, "we can balance the mistakes of the spectator and the actor against each other, for the actor is always more or less betrayed by his feelings and the spectator is deceived by action." The actor always thinks: "I did it for the best." The spectator thinks, like your own poet:

Of course he did it for the best;
What could he do it for?
But did he do it? That's the test.
I want to know no more.

It is the novelist who can bring to us the whole dossier. He gives us at once the actor's opinion of himself, the spectator's opinion of the actor, and a third opinion built up out of the other two, which, far from being a super-added judgment, is the very act of creation....The closer one looks at the question, the more clearly one sees that a character in a novel exists only if there is a correspondence between his inner life and his outward life, the one calling the other into being or both being created simultaneously, according to the preferences and the methods of the novelist[1].

It is in this impossibility of attaining to a synthesis of the inner life and the outward that the inferiority of the biographer to the novelist lies. The biographer quite clearly sees Peel, say, seated on his bench while his opponents overwhelm him with perhaps undeserved censure. He sees him motionless, miserable, his head bent on his breast. He asks himself: "What is he thinking?" and he knows nothing. Sometimes he has materials. Sometimes even he has more than the novelist, but materials are not everything. Think of the scholars who study prehistory; they have materials; they discover in the ground a considerable number of polished stone axes, of little pebbles in the form of spear-heads and of painted bisons on the walls of grottos. It is not flint axes or knives that they lack; they have only too many. It is because they have four thousand flints and two thousand axes that the museums of

[1] Fernandez.

prehistory are so wearisome and that one comes away from them with the impression of having learnt little of what prehistoric man really was. Like Mr Chesterton, we have some difficulty in believing that there ever existed a being for whom human life was not a tissue of desires and fears and passions, but a long exercise which consisted in shaping small pebbles and in painting bisons. Mr Kipling teaches us much more when (without any of the museum apparatus) he depicts the prehistoric tribes for us. In the same way the biographer may have a hundred and fifty letters written by a statesman, or he may have fifteen hundred. It may be useful to print them, to establish for us documentary stores of this kind; but it is not from such museum collections that a living image can emerge. Such collections must exist; but we must not live among them. "History," says the philosopher Alain, "is empty of content because it condemns itself to accept the passions which each man avows. It moves in an abstract order of things and real life escapes it." On the one hand it makes a collection of all the fragments of axes, even when they resemble each other; on the other, when it cannot find any axes, it says that there are none—but there is no proof of that.

In his lectures last year Mr Forster showed you very clearly the difference between a character in fiction and a character in biography:

> If a character in a novel is exactly like Queen Victoria—not rather like but exactly like—then it actually is Queen Victoria, and the novel, or all of it that the character touches, becomes a memoir. A memoir is history, it is based on evidence. A novel is based on evidence + or $-x$, the unknown quantity being the temperament of the novelist, and the unknown quantity always modifies the effect of the evidence, and sometimes transforms it entirely.

The historian deals with actions, and with the characters of men only so far as he can deduce them from their actions. He is quite as much concerned with character as the novelist, but he can only know of its existence when it shows on the surface. If Queen Victoria had not said, "We are not amused," her neighbours at table would not have known she was not amused, and her ennui could never have been announced to the public. She might have frowned, so that they would have deduced her state from that—looks and gestures are also historical evidence. But if she remained impassive—what would anyone know? The hidden life is, by definition, hidden. The hidden life that appears in external signs is hidden no longer, has entered the realm of action. And it is the function of the novelist to reveal the hidden life at its source: to tell us more about Queen Victoria than could be known, and thus to produce a character who is not the Queen Victoria of History.

May I add "who is not the Queen Victoria of history, but is more like Queen Victoria than the Queen Victoria of history"?

"To get a truer idea of the importance and of the atmosphere of the Revolutionary and Napoleonic era," writes Mr Rowse, "we must leave the historians for the novelists, we must read Tolstoy's *War and Peace* and Hardy's *Dynasts*," and it is almost true. I say "almost," because Tolstoy did not understand the greatness, the real, human greatness of Napoleon; but he did know how to make the Emperor Alexander, Napoleon himself, and Koutouzov real living beings. What artifice did he employ? Well, in the first place, they are seen through the medium of heroes of novels (Boris, Prince André) with whom we naturally identify ourselves; secondly, Tolstoy, who was a visionary, knew at any moment what were the gestures and the facial expressions of his historical heroes. It is true that these gestures and expressions are themselves historical facts. Yes, when they are known—but that happens very rarely. What historian, for instance, would be justified in writing, in the same form as Tolstoy, an account such as this of Napoleon's visit to the Russian army?

"Sire, I crave your leave to give the Legion of Honour to the bravest of your soldiers," said a clear voice, pronouncing each syllable very distinctly. It was the small figure of Bonaparte that spoke, looking up straight into the eyes of the Tsar, who listened attentively and smiled at him as he nodded assent.

"To the man who has displayed greatest courage in this war!" added Napoleon with a coolness which Rostov bore ill and, as he spoke, he looked calmly at the ranks of the Russian soldiers, who stood at the present and kept their eyes immovably fixed on the figure of the Tsar.

"Will your Majesty permit me to consult the Colonel?" said Alexander, stepping towards Prince Kozlovsky, who was in command of the battalion. Bonaparte with some difficulty removed the glove from his small white hand. It was torn and he threw it away. An aide-de-camp sprang forward to pick it up....Napoleon turned his head imperceptibly and stretched out his small, chubby hand as if to take something. The members of his staff, at once guessing what he wanted, hastily murmured to each other and passed a small object from hand to hand. A page, the very one whom Nicolas had seen with Boris, sprang forward and, with a respectful salute, laid in the outstretched hand a cross with a red ribbon. Napoleon took it without looking at it and advanced towards Lazarev who with wide eyes continued to gaze fixedly at his emperor. Casting a glance at the Tsar to convince him that what he was about to do was an act of graciousness prompted by himself, Napoleon placed his hand which held the cross on the soldier's breast, as though his touch alone should suffice to make the soldier happy for all time in having thus been singled out for decoration.

No biographer could have given this vivid impression of the emperor; no document would have enabled him to show Napoleon stretching out his small chubby hand or casting a glance at the Tsar, unless it had happened that some eye-witness had made a note of such attitudes and gestures for him. But, at nearly all the great moments, such eye-witnesses, with the power of using their eyes, are wanting. It is the same with Koutouzov when Dologhov says to the general in the course of a review: "Have the goodness to give me the opportunity of blotting out my fault and of giving proof of my devotion to the emperor and to Russia." Koutouzov turned and made towards his carriage with an air of disgust. These banal phrases, always in the same form, bored him, wearied him. "What," he thought, "is the good of replying in the same old strain? What is the good of these old and eternal repetitions?" Two phrases only, but two phrases which make us understand all the old man's despairing serenity, his weariness of the monotony of life; two phrases which would have been forbidden to the historian since he would have had no document by which to justify them.

Such conclusions offer little encouragement to the biographer. Must he then admit himself to be defeated by the novelist? May he, in certain respects, profit by the novelist's experience and endeavour to utilise his technique? Has he not, on his part, certain advantages which the novelist lacks? Such are the questions which I should like to propound to-day, taking one by one and examining from the biographer's point of view the various topics treated last year by Mr Forster from the point of view of the novelist. Mr Forster first dealt at some length with what he calls the "pattern" of a novel, or, if you like, that quality of arrangement which, by giving to the novel a simple form, makes it an intelligible work of art.

At first sight the biographer seems, in this respect, to be in a much more difficult position than the novelist. Except in those rare cases in which he is writing the history of a man whose life happens to have constructed itself, he is obliged to take over a shapeless mass, made up of unequal fragments prolonged in every direction by isolated groups of events which lead nowhere. There are deserts in every life, and the desert must be depicted if we are to give a fair and complete idea of the country. It is true that these long periods of empty monotony sometimes throw up the colour of the livelier periods into greater relief. Balzac was not afraid of deserts in his novels. But the biographer will never have the luck to find a life perfectly grouped round a single passion like that of Père Grandet, or of Père Goriot, or even that of M. de Charlus. Thus the biographer has greater difficulty than the novelist in composition. But he has one compensation: to be compelled to take over the form of a work ready-made is almost always a source of power to the artist. It is painful, it makes his task more difficult; but at the same time it is from this struggle between the mind and the matter that resists it that a masterpiece is born. When Michael Angelo and other great sculptors of the Renaissance were given curiously-shaped blocks of marble by their patrons and their tyrants, they had to obey orders and make the best of them. Very often it was from these strange forms that the loveliest designs were made; the resistance of the marble forced the artist to invent. Some of the most felicitous word-pictures have been the result of the limitations imposed by the formal rigidity of classical verse. The trouble about certain novels is that their construction is too free. Being at liberty to fashion his characters as he likes, the novelist makes them abstract beings, well fitted to illustrate an argument or to take their place in the geometrical arrangement of a preconceived framework. It is thus that one gets what Mr Forster calls the "hour-glass" pattern of Anatole France's *Thaïs*, a good example of a novel that is highly intelligent, but just a little too clever.

After badly constructed books there is one thing even more dangerous, and that is books that are too well constructed. This excess of construction springs from an excess of freedom. If you study the history of the novel in England or elsewhere, you will see that the best novelists often impose restraints upon themselves and proceed to search for situations and documents in real life just as a biographer would do. Meredith borrowed many of his characters from real life; Tolstoy, in *War and Peace*, utilised the history of his own family; Maurice Baring told me that he took the theme of *Cat's Cradle* from the obituary notice of an old lady in a newspaper. Gide, in *Le Journal des faux monnayeurs*, makes it clear that he prefers to accept an odd fact as a *datum* and not to construct it *a priori*.

In my view, a series of events thus borrowed from actual life and then transmuted by the novelist's art will always ring truer than entirely imaginary events. The absurdity of truth is magnificent and well-nigh inimitable and a man must have genius to be as flagrantly absurd as God. But the novelist, even if he takes over from real life certain combinations of events which accord with his plans and his passions, must always cut out with the surgeon's knife the growth of parasitic events; whereas the biographer is doomed to live with his malady. He must do some work of composition, of course, or else he ceases to be an artist; but it must be more by means of the painter's or of the poet's rhythm.

Now let us turn to what Mr Forster calls "the story." He explains, quite rightly, that the first quality of a novel must be to compel the reader to want to listen, and to listen to the end. "Scheherazade," he says, "only survived because she managed to keep the king wondering what would happen next." Would Scheherazade have survived if she had written biographies? Does a biography form as continuous, as interesting, a story as a novel? That depends on the choice of subject. The story of Disraeli presents very precisely all the characteristics of a tale of *The Thousand and One Nights*. It is a tale because self-confidence and audacity triumph in the end; nor is the good fairy, Queen Victoria, wanting; further, as in *The Beauty in the Sleeping Wood*, we come upon the whole company of fairies: Mary Ann, Mrs Austen, Lady Dorothy Nevill, Lady Chesterfield, Lady Bradford. Yes, I think that with Disraeli Scheherazade would have survived.

Certainly she would have survived with a Life of Meredith. For Meredith's Life is as instinct with passion as a novel and is even constructed like a novel—his childhood in the tailor's shop, the first marriage which was a failure, his pure, romantic love for a young girl, Janet Duff-Gordon; then the successful second marriage and a period of serenity. Yes, certainly with a Life of Meredith, Scheherazade would have survived. With others, however, life is a colourless affair, unrolling itself without any great surprises and ill fitted to maintain the reader's interest. Certain lives which contain some interesting episodes contain too few of them and are too monotonous to adapt themselves to a continuous narrative.

Consider a character like Mrs Siddons. At first sight one exclaims, "How interesting she must be!" One comes upon a certain number of picturesque scenes. The character itself is a beautiful one. Then one realises that all the Lives of Mrs Siddons so far written are dull, because the life of the actress is fundamentally monotonous.

There are biographies which are boring and one must beware of writing them. At the same time it is true that there are novels which are boring, and that novelists have written them.

Let us pass on to *Characters*. Mr Forster explains that we must distinguish carefully between man as he is in the novel and man as he is in real life—the two distinct species, *Homo Fictus* and *Homo Sapiens*.

Homo Fictus is more elusive than his cousin....

Still one can say a little about him. He is generally born off, he is capable of dying on, he wants little food or sleep, he is tirelessly occupied with human relationships.

Homo Sapiens is primarily occupied with food and work, and is occupied with love, if at all, for one or two hours a day.

Homo Biographicus is a third species. What distinguishes him from the other two is that he is much more in action. Homo Sapiens, the man in real life, sometimes spends several days in idling or in losing himself in a vague reverie; he plays golf; he chats with his friends. Homo Biographicus is always in action; he is writing letters, or governing empires (or trying to govern them), or running after women or deserting them; he is a being of quite incredible activity.

His mode of expression is very different from that of Homo Fictus, whom in other respects he resembles. Homo Fictus talks a great deal or indulges in meditation in the form of a talk with himself which—by a miracle peculiar to the novel—we are able to hear when, with the novelist, we occupy the observation-post of God Almighty. Homo Biographicus, on the other hand, talks very little with his fellows and never thinks when he is alone. He writes letters and often keeps a diary. If he writes no letters and does not keep a diary, it is a bad mark against him, and furthermore he is punished by the fact that he practically ceases to exist. It is true that Homo Sapiens also writes letters, but his letters are of no great importance. Very often he doesn't believe in them; he knows their proper value and would be astonished if anyone should regard them as authoritative. Homo Biographicus writes a letter and always believes what he writes—at any rate, that is the impression we receive from all who are concerned with him.

Homo Biographicus is treated with much greater severity than Homo Sapiens. Homo Sapiens is continually contradicting himself, is successively or simultaneously in love with several women; he begins life as an anarchist and ends as a conservative or *vice versa.* We forgive him because we do not consider his career from one point of view only; we see him changing imperceptibly and consequently we have time to get used to his successive variations. Homo Biographicus, on the other hand, is put together in two or three hundred pages under the eyes of strict judges and we condemn him as soon as he contradicts himself. When, like Chateaubriand, he writes three love-letters to three different women in the same day we condemn him as faithless and inconstant. You see that life is a difficult thing for him.

We may add that it is perhaps with him as with the monstrous reptiles of the Secondary Epoch; he is a species in process of disappearance. He was primarily made up, as we have seen, of correspondence and diaries; modern life, moreover, tends, by its rush as well as by its more rapid means of communication, to obliterate all the writing on paper which forms the flesh and blood of Homo Biographicus. The most romantic passages in life to-day take place over the telephone. A modern Byron and Caroline Lamb would leave absolutely no trace of their conflict. The only man who still writes is the statesman, in order to "fix responsibility," but he writes with the aid of a typewriter and we have already seen—in a biography of President Wilson—the spectacle of an author obliged to publish shorthand notes in order to illustrate his book. Verily, the life of Homo Biographicus seems to be precarious.

And yet, and yet...when he is well cared for, Homo Biographicus can live. He is like those delicate plants which need a thousand little attentions, but repay such attentions by the charm of their foliage and the beauty of their blossom. When Homo Biographicus comes into the hands of a clever doctor, the doctor can, by means of suitable injections, endow him with that inner life which characterises Homo Fictus—and that without injury to truth.

Must we, in conclusion, attempt to write *Plutarch, or the Future of Biography*? Must I confess that in my own view the future will not be very different from the present? There is no such thing as progress in literature. Tennyson is not greater than Homer, Proust is not greater than Montaigne, Strachey is not greater than Boswell. They are different. Literature follows a rhythmical course rather than a continuous line. We shall come once more into periods of social and religious certainty in which few intimate biographies will be written and panegyrics will take their place.

Subsequently we shall again reach a period of doubt and despair in which biography will re-appear as a source of confidence and re-assurance.

Whatever forms biography may assume in the

future, it will always be a difficult form of art. We demand of it the scrupulosity of science and the enchantments of art, the perceptible truth of the novel and the learned falsehoods of history. Much prudence and tact are required to concoct this unstable mixture. Carlyle said that a well-written life was almost as rare as a well-spent one, thus showing himself as much an optimist in his criticism as he was a pessimist in his ethics. A well-written life is a much rarer thing than a well-spent one. But, however difficult biography may be, it merits the devotion of our toil and of our emotions. The cult of the hero is as old as mankind. It sets before men examples which are lofty but not inaccessible, astonishing but not incredible, and it is this double quality which makes it the most convincing of art-forms and the most human of religions.

INDEX

INDEX

INDEX

For EU product safety concerns, contact us at Calle de José Abascal, 56–1°, 28003 Madrid, Spain or eugpsr@cambridge.org.

www.ingramcontent.com/pod-product-compliance
Ingram Content Group UK Ltd.
Pitfield, Milton Keynes, MK11 3LW, UK
UKHW020316140625
459647UK00018B/1898

* 9 7 8 1 1 0 7 4 3 7 5 8 6 *